LINQ for Visual VB 2005

FABIO CLAUDIO FERRACCHIATI

firstPress™

LINQ for VB 2005

Copyright © 2007 by Fabio Claudio Ferracchiati

ISBN-13: 978-1-59059-840-5

ISBN-10: 1-59059-840-7

Printed and bound in the United States of America (POD)

Lead Editor: James Huddleston

Technical Reviewer: Vidya Vrat Agarwal

Editorial Board: Steve Anglin, Ewan Buckingham, Gary Cornell, Jason Gilmore, Jonathan Gennick, Jonathan Hassell, James Huddleston, Chris Mills, Matthew Moodie, Dominic Shakeshaft, Jim Sumser, Matt Wade
Project Manager: Kylie Johnston

Project Manager: Kylie Johnston

Copy Edit Manager: Nicole Flores

Copy Editor: Candace English

Assistant Production Director: Kari Brooks-Copony

Compositor: Richard Ables

Cover Designer: Kurt Krames

Manufacturing Director: Tom Debolski

Distributed to the book trade worldwide by Springer-Verlag New York, Inc., 233 Spring Street, 6th Floor, New York, NY 10013. Phone 1-800-SPRINGER, fax 201-348-4505, e-mail orders-ny@springer-sbm.com, or visit http://www.springeronline.com.

For information on translations, please contact Apress directly at 2560 Ninth Street, Suite 219, Berkeley, CA 94710. Phone 510-549-5930, fax 510-549-5939, e-mail info@apress.com, or visit http://www.apress.com.

The source code for this book is available to readers at http://www.apress.com in the Source Code/ Download section.

To Simona: "Tu ed io per sempre"—05/08/2005

Contents

About the Author

FABIO CLAUDIO FERRACCHIATI is a senior consultant and a senior analyst/developer using Microsoft technologies. He works for Brain Force (www.brainforce.com) in its Italian branch (www.brainforce.it). He is a Microsoft Certified Solution Developer for .NET, a Microsoft Certified Application Developer for .NET, and a Microsoft Certified Professional, and a prolific author and technical reviewer. Over the past ten years he's written articles for Italian and international magazines and coauthored more than ten books on a variety of computer topics, including *LINQ for Visual C# 2005* (Apress 2006). You can find his blog on LINQ at www.ferracchiati.com.

About the Technical Reviewer

VIDYA VRAT AGARWAL is a Microsoft .NET Purist and an MCTS, MCPD, MCT, MCSD.NET, MCAD.NET, and MCSD certified technician. He works with Lionbridge (NASDAQ: LIOX) and his business card reads Subject Matter Expert (SME). He is also a lifetime member of the Computer Society of India (CSI). He started working on Microsoft.NET with its beta release. He has been involved in software development, evangelism, consultation, corporate training, and T3 programs on Microsoft .NET for various employers and corporate clients.

He lives with his beloved wife and lovely daughter Vamika ("Pearly"). He believes that nothing will turn into a reality without them. He is the follower of the concept No Pain, No Gain and believes that his wife is his greatest strength. He is a bibliophile; when he is not working on technical stuff he likes to play with his one-year-old daughter and also likes reading spiritual and occult science books. He blogs at `http://dotnetpassion.blogspot.com`.

Acknowledgments

There are many people I'd like to thank! Every person working for Apress deserves special thanks for their kindness. In particular, my historical "virtual" friend, Ewan Buckingham, who suggested I write this book, and Jim Huddleston, who gave me support, tips, and technical suggestions. Thanks to Kylie Johnston for her great work behind the scenes. Thanks to Vidya Vrat Agarwal, the technical reviewer, who helped me refine my book. I'd like to thank my friend Walter Folli, a very smart analyst/developer, who helped me better understand my ORM issues. Finally, a great thanks to Candace English, who helped me to improve the English grammar of my book .

Introduction

Over the past 20 years object-oriented programming languages have evolved to become the premier tools for enterprise application development. They've been augmented by frameworks, APIs, and rapid application-development tools. Yet what's been missing is a way to intimately tie object-oriented programs to relational databases (and other data that doesn't exist as objects). The object paradigm is conceptually different from the relational one and this creates significant impedance between the objects programs use and the tables where data resides. ADO.NET provides a convenient interface to relational data, but not an object-oriented one. For example, this pseudocode would be really cool:

```
' A class representing a table of employees
Dim e As New Employees()

' Set the row identifier to one
e.ID = 1

' Retrieve the row where ID=1
e.Retrieve()

' Change the Name column value to Alan
e.Name = "Alan"

' Modify the database data
e.Upate()
```

The pseudocode shows an object-oriented approach to data management; no query or SQL statement is visible to developers. You need to think about only what you have to do, not how to do it. This approach to combining object-oriented and relational technologies has been called the Object-Relational Mapping (ORM) model.

Although Microsoft has embedded ORM capabilities in its Dynamics CRM 3.0 application server and should soon do the same in ADO.NET 3.0, it doesn't yet provide this programming model to .NET developers. To run a simple SQL query, ADO.NET programmers have to store the SQL in a Command object, associate the Command with a Connection object and execute it on that Connection object, then use a DataReader or other object to retrieve the result set. For example, the following code is necessary to retrieve the single row accessed in the pseudocode presented earlier.

```
' Specify the connection to the DB
Dim c As New SqlConnection(…)

' Open the connection
c.Open()


' Specify the SQL Command
Dim cmd As New SqlCommand( _
    "SELECT _
        * _
    FROM _
        Employees e _
    WHERE _
        e.ID = @p0 _
")

' Add a value to the parameter
cmd.Parameters.AddWithValue("@p0", 1)

' Excute the command
Dim dr As DataReader = c.Execute(cmd)

' Retrieve the Name column value
While (dr.Read())
    Dim name As String = dr.GetString(0)
End While

' Update record using another Command object
…

' Close the connection
c.Close()
```

Not only is this a lot more code than the ORM code, but there's also no way for the VB compiler to check our query against our use of the data it returns. When we retrieve the employee's name we have to know the column's position in the database table to find it in the result. It's a common mistake to retrieve the wrong column and get a type exception or bad data at run time.

ADO.NET moved toward ORM with strongly typed DataSets. But we still have to write the same kind of code, using a DataAdapter instead of a Command object. The DataAdapter contains four Command objects, one for each database operation-SELECT, DELETE, INSERT, and UPDATE-and we have fill the correct one with the appropriate SQL code.

.NET can also handle XML and nonrelational data sources, but then we have to know other ways to query information, such as XPath or XQuery. SQL and XML can be made to work together but only by shifting mental gears at the right time.

What Is LINQ?

At the Microsoft Professional Developers Conference (PDC) 2005, Anders Hejlsberg and his team presented a new approach, *Language-Integrated Query* (LINQ), that unifies the way data can be retrieved in .NET. LINQ provides a uniform way to retrieve data from any object that implements the IEnumerable(Of T) interface. With LINQ, arrays, collections, relational data, and XML are all potential data sources.

Why LINQ?

With LINQ, you can use the same syntax to retrieve data from any data source:

```
Dim query = From e in employees _
Where e.id = 1 _
Select e.name
```

This is not pseudocode; this is LINQ syntax, and it's very similar to SQL. The LINQ team's goal was not to add yet another way to access data, but to provide a native, integrated set of instructions to query any kind of data source. Using VB keywords, we can write data access code as part of VB, and the VB compiler will be able to enforce type safety and even logical consistency. LINQ provides a rich set of instructions to implement complex queries that support data aggregation, joins, sorting, and much more.

Figure 1 presents an overview of LINQ functionality. The top level shows the languages that provide native support for LINQ. Currently, only C# 3.0 and Visual Basic 9.0 offer complete support for LINQ.

The middle level represents the three main parts of the LINQ project:

LINQ to Objects is an API that provides methods that represent a set of standard query operators (SQOs) to retrieve data from any object whose class implements the IEnumerable(Of T) interface. These queries are performed against in-memory data.

LINQ to ADO.NET augments SQOs to work against relational data. It is composed of three parts (which appear at the bottom level of Figure 1): **LINQ to SQL** (formerly DLinq) is use to query relational databases such as Microsoft SQL Server. **LINQ to DataSet** supports queries by using ADO.NET data sets and data tables. **LINQ to Entities** is a Microsoft ORM solution, allowing developers to use Entities (an ADO.NET 3.0 feature) to declaratively specify the structure of business objects and use LINQ to query them.

LINQ to XML (formerly XLinq) not only augments SQOs but also includes a host of XML-specific features for XML document creation and queries.

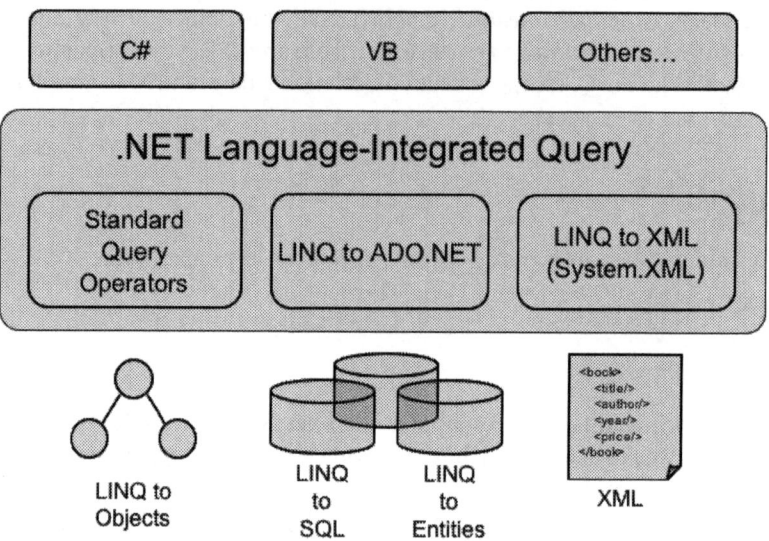

Figure 1. Data domains in which LINQ adds functionality

▮**Note** I don't cover LINQ to Entities because the ADO.NET Entity Framework is an ADO.NET 3.0 feature, and is not yet as mature as other technologies that can be used with LINQ.

Now let's see what you need to work with LINQ.

What You Need to Use LINQ

LINQ is a combination of extensions to .NET languages and class libraries that support them. To use it, you'll need the following:

- LINQ, which is available from the LINQ Project website at http://msdn.microsoft.com/data/ref/linq. I've used the May 2006 CTP for this book.

- NET 2.0 running on Windows 2000 (Service Pack 4), Windows Server 2003, Windows XP Pro (Service Pack 2), or Windows Vista.

- To write VB programs using LINQ, you need either Visual Studio 2005 or Visual Basic 2005 Express Edition.

- To use LINQ to ADO.NET, you need SQL Server 2005, SQL Server 2005 Express Edition, or SQL Server 2000.

- If you want to use LINQ with .NET 3.0 (originally WinFX), you need the WinFX Runtime Beta 2.

Resources

There's a lot of good material available about LINQ:

- The LINQ May 2006 CTP includes a complete set of documentation.

- The main LINQ Project site (http://msdn.microsoft.com/data/ref/linq) includes a Forums section where thousands of developers discuss LINQ, ask for support, and report bugs.

- At http://shop.ecompanystore.com/mseventdvd/MSD_Shop.asp you can order the DVD that contains full sessions from PDC 2005, where LINQ was unveiled.

- My blog on LINQ development at www.ferracchiati.com.

- On the Channel 9 site (http://channel9.msdn.com), Anders Hejlsberg and his team are often interviewed about LINQ issues and development.

What's Next?

This book contains three chapters, each dedicated to one of the main aspects of LINQ. The content assumes you're comfortable with VB generics and delegates. You can learn and use LINQ without a deep understanding of these topics, but the more you know about them the faster you'll grasp LINQ's concepts and implementation.

Chapter 1 discusses LINQ to Objects, with a sample program that illustrates its major functionality.

Chapter 2 provides a complete description of LINQ to SQL (LINQ's components for accessing relational data) and its great functionalities. A rich sample program demonstrates its features.

Chapter 3 covers LINQ to XML (LINQ's components for accessing XML data). You'll see how to generate XML from queries and interrogate XML documents to retrieve data by using LINQ syntax.

CHAPTER 1

LINQ to Objects

In this chapter we'll study LINQ fundamentals by exploring its features for querying in-memory objects. We'll start with some simple examples to get an idea of what programming with LINQ to Objects involves, then we'll look at examples for all of LINQ's standard query operators.

Introduction

Data domains are different from object domains. When we deal with objects like arrays and collections, we use iteration to retrieve their elements. If we're looking for a particular element based on its content rather than its index, we have to use a loop and process each element individually. For example, for an array of strings there is no built-in method to retrieve all elements whose length is equal to a particular value.

   LINQ addresses this challenge by providing a uniform way to access data from any data source using familiar syntax. It lets us focus on working with data rather than on accessing it.

   LINQ to Objects can be used with any class that implements the IEnumerable(Of T) interface. Let's look at how it works.

A Simple VB LINQ to Objects Program

Listing 1-1 is a console program snippet that uses LINQ to Objects to display a specific element in an array.

Listing 1-1. Using LINQ to Objects with List(Of T)

```
          Dim people As List(Of Person)

people = New List(Of Person) { _
    {ID := 1, IDRole := 1, LastName := "Anderson", FirstName := "Brad"}, _
    {ID := 2, IDRole := 2, LastName := "Gray", FirstName := "Tom"} _
}

Dim query = From p In people _
```

```
Where p.ID = 1 _
Select p
```

```
ObjectDumper.Write(query)
```

In Listing 1-1 you define a collection of Person objects and insert a couple of elements. List(Of T) is a generic class that implements IEnumerable(Of T), so it's suitable for LINQ querying.

Next you declare a variable, query, to hold the result of a LINQ query. Don't worry about the Dim keyword without the variable's type definition right now; it will be discussed later in this chapter, in "Implicitly Typed Local Variables."

You initialize query to a LINQ's *query expression*. The From clause specifies a data source. The variable p represents an object in the people collection. The Where clause specifies a condition for selecting from the data source. You want to retrieve just the person whose ID equals 1, so you specify a Boolean expression, p.ID = 1. Finally, the Select clause specifies what Person data you're interested in retrieving.

The ObjectDumper class is a convenient utility for producing formatted output. It has only one method, Write(), which has three overloads.

When you run the program you'll see the result in Figure 1-1.

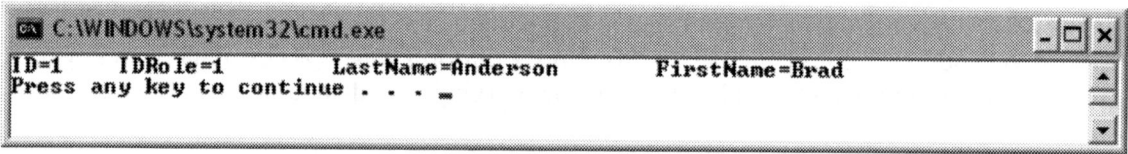

Figure 1-1. Using LINQ to query a list

This very simple example uses some new features from VB 9.0. The first is a query expression that is similar to the one used in SQL and allows developers to use query-language syntax that they are already accustomed to. When the compiler finds a query expression in the code, it transforms that expression into VB method calls. Listing 1-2 shows how the query expression in Listing 1-1 would be transformed.

Listing 1-2. Transformed LINQ to Object Code

```
Sub Listing1_2()
    Dim query = people.Where(AddressOf F)

  ObjectDumper.Write(query)
End Sub

Function F(ByVal people As Person) As Boolean
```

```
    Return people.ID = 1
End Function
```

The From keyword has been removed, leaving just the collection, people, against which to perform the query. The Where clause has been transformed into a method call: Where(Of T)(). This method accepts a delegate function where we have to specify the filtering condition. Automatically, the compiler has created a function F and has inserted the filtering condition (ID = 1). The Select method has been removed from the query because we have said to retrieve all the fields from the Person class.

You may wonder how this is possible. VB doesn't provide the Where method for the List(Of T) class. Moreover, LINQ runs on .NET 2.0 and installing LINQ doesn't replace any .NET 2.0 assemblies. The answer is extension methods.

Extension Methods

As the name implies, extension methods extend existing .NET types with new methods. For example, by using extension methods with a String, it's possible to add a new method that converts every space in a String to an underscore. Listing 1-3 provides an example of an extension method.

Listing 1-3. An Extension Method

```
<Extension()> _
Public Class Extensions

    <Extension()> _
    Public Shared Function SpaceToUnderscore(ByVal source As String) As String
        Dim cArray As Char() = source.ToCharArray()
        Dim result As String = String.Empty

        For Each c As Char In cArray
            If Char.IsWhiteSpace(c) Then
                result = result & "_"
            Else
                result = result & c
            End If
        Next

        Return result
    End Function
End Class
```

```
Sub Listing1_3()
    Dim s As String = "this is a test"
    Console.WriteLine(s.SpaceToUnderscore())
End Sub
```

Here you define an extension method, SpaceToUnderscore(). To specify an extension method you insert the attribute <Extension()> before the method's prototype definition. Note that the method must be Shared. You can use SpaceToUnderscore() just like any other String method, just importing the namespace that includes the new extended method.

Figure 1-2 shows the result of executing this method.

Figure 1-2. Calling an extension method

The Where(Of T) method that the Where clause has been transformed into is an extension method defined for the IEnumerable(Of T) interface. It is in the System.Query namespace.

Note ➡ The May 2006 CTP LINQ installation includes the Sequence.cs file (in the Docs directory). This file contains the source code for all the extension methods in the System.Query namespace. Sadly, there isn't a VB version of this file.

Simply by adding the new System.Query namespace, you can use LINQ with any type that implements IEnumerable(Of T). You don't have to install a new version of .NET or replace any existing assemblies. You do have to consider a couple of things when implementing and using extension methods, however:

- If you have an extension method and an instance method with the same signature, priority is given to the instance method.

- Properties, events, and operators are not extendable.

Lambda Expressions

VB 9.0 doesn't support lambda expressions. They are a new C# 3.0 feature that simplifies coding delegates and anonymous methods.

Lambda expressions allow us to write functions that can be passed as arguments to methods, such as to supply predicates for subsequent evaluation. For example, using C# 3.0 and the Where standard operator we can specify a lambda expression to define the filtering condition in this way:

```
people.Where(p => p.ID);
```

You could use code like that in Listing 1-4 to obtain the same result, but the lambda expression syntax is simpler. In fact, it allows us to not specify a delegate function, and instead to declare its body directly in the lambda expression constructor. (By the way, using VB and a bit more effort, we can obtain the same result.)

Listing 1-4. Alternative to Lambda Expression Syntax

```
Dim predicate As New Func(Of Person, Boolean)(AddressOf wherePredicate)
Dim query = people.Where(predicate)

ObjectDumper.Write(query)
```

In the wherePredicate method we can specify the where condition as shown in the following code snippet:

```
Public Function wherePredicate(ByVal p As Person) As Boolean
    Return p.ID = 1
End Function
```

In this code we have used a Func(Of A0, T) method provided by the System.Query namespace that accepts an IEnumerable(Of T) collection parameter and returns the T type. The System.Query namespace provides five Func() methods' versions to accept up to four input collections.

Object Initialization Expressions

The code in Listing 1-1 used another VB 9.0 feature called *object initialization expressions*:

```
people As List(Of Person) = New List(Of Person) { _
    {ID := 1, IDRole := 1, LastName := "Anderson", FirstName := "Brad"}, _
    {ID := 2, IDRole := 2, LastName := "Gray", FirstName := "Tom"} _
}
```

Just like an array initializer, an object initialization expression allows us to initialize a new object without calling its constructor and without setting its properties. Let's look at an example in Listing 1-5.

Listing 1-5. Using an Object Initialization Expression

```
Sub Listing1_5()
    ' The standard object creation and initialization
    Dim p1 As New Person()
    p1.FirstName = "Brad"
    p1.LastName = "Anderson"
    ObjectDumper.Write(p1)

    Dim p2 = New Person {FirstName := "Tom", LastName := "Gray"}
    ObjectDumper.Write(p2)
End Sub
```

With object initialization expressions you can create an object directly and set its properties using just one statement. However, you can also write code *without* specifying the class you are instantiating. See the code snippet in Listing 1-6 and focus your attention on the bold text.

Listing 1-6. Using the New Anonymous Types Feature

```
Dim query = From p In people _
    Where p.ID = 1 _
        Select New {p.FirstName, p.LastName}

ObjectDumper.Write(query)
```

It's not an error; it's another new feature called *anonymous types*, and I'll cover it next.

Anonymous Types

In Listing 1-6, note that no type was specified after the New keyword in the object initialization expression. The compiler created a locally scoped anonymous type for us.

Anonymous types let us work with query results on the fly without having to explicitly define classes to represent them. When the compiler encountered

```
Select New { p.FirstName, p.LastName }
```

in Listing 1-6 it transparently created a new class with two properties, one for each parameter (see Listing 1-7).

Listing 1-7. A Class for an Anonymous Type

```
Public Class _Anonymous_Listing1_6_7A_13
    Implements IEquatable(Of _Anonymous_Listing1_6_7A_13)
```

```
' Methods
Public Sub New()
Public Function Equals(ByVal val As _Anonymous_Listing1_6_7A_13) As Boolean Implements
IEquatable(Of _Anonymous_Listing1_6_7A_13).Equals
    Public Overrides Function Equals(ByVal obj As Object) As Boolean
    Public Overrides Function GetHashCode() As Integer
    Public Overrides Function ToString() As String

' Properties
Public Property FirstName As String
Public Property LastName As String

' Fields
Private _FirstName As String
Private _LastName As String
End Class
```

As you can see in Listing 1-7, the property names are taken directly from the fields specified in the Person class. However, you can indicate the properties for the anonymous type explicitly using the following syntax:

```
New { firstN := p.FirstName, lastN := p.LastName }
```

Now to use the anonymous type in the code you have to respect the new names and the case-sensitive syntax. For example, to print the full name you would use the following:

```
Console.WriteLine("Full Name = {0} {1}", query.firstN, query.lastN)
```

Keep in mind that the anonymous type itself cannot be referenced from the code. How is it possible to access the results of a query if you don't know the name of the new type? The compiler handles this for you by inferring the type. We'll look at this next.

Implicitly Typed Local Variables

When the compiler sees Dim without a variable's type declaration, it implicitly defines the type of the variable based on the type of expression that initializes the variable. While its use is mandatory with anonymous types, it can be applied even in other cases, such as the following:

- Dim i = 5 is equivalent to Dim i As Integer = 5

- Dim s = "this is a string" is equivalent to Dim s As String = "this is a string"

An implicitly typed local variable must have an initializer. For example, the following declaration is invalid:

Dim s ' wrong definition, no initializer

As you can imagine, implicit typing is really useful for complex query results because it eliminates the need to define a custom type for each result.

Note ➡ Implicitly typed local variables cannot be used as method parameters.

Query Evaluation Time

It is important to understand when the query is evaluated at run time. In Listing 1-1 nothing happens in query execution until the ObjectDumper's Write method is called. Listing 1-8 looks at the code behind this method:

Listing 1-8. The Core Method of the ObjectDumper Helper Class

```
Private Sub WriteObject(ByVal prefix As String, ByVal o As Object)
    If (((o Is Nothing) OrElse TypeOf o Is ValueType) OrElse TypeOf o Is String) Then
        Me.WriteIndent
        Me.Write(prefix)
        Me.WriteValue(o)
        Me.WriteLine
    ElseIf TypeOf o Is IEnumerable Then
        Dim obj1 As Object
        For Each obj1 In DirectCast(o, IEnumerable)
            If (TypeOf obj1 Is IEnumerable AndAlso Not TypeOf obj1 Is String) Then
                Me.WriteIndent
                Me.Write(prefix)
                Me.Write("...")
                Me.WriteLine
                If (Me.level < Me.depth) Then
                    Me.level += 1
                    Me.WriteObject(prefix, obj1)
                    Me.level -= 1
                End If
            Else
                Me.WriteObject(prefix, obj1)
            End If
        Next
```

```vb
Else
    Dim infoArray1 As MemberInfo() = o.GetType.GetMembers((BindingFlags.Public Or _
                                                            BindingFlags.Instance))

Me.WriteIndent
Me.Write(prefix)
Dim flag1 As Boolean = False
Dim info1 As MemberInfo
For Each info1 In infoArray1
    Dim info2 As FieldInfo = TryCast(info1,FieldInfo)
    Dim info3 As PropertyInfo = TryCast(info1,PropertyInfo)
    If ((Not info2 Is Nothing) OrElse (Not info3 Is Nothing)) Then
        If flag1 Then
            Me.WriteTab
        Else
            flag1 = True
        End If
        Me.Write(info1.Name)
        Me.Write("=")
        Dim type1 As Type = _
                IIf((Not info2 Is Nothing), info2.FieldType, info3.PropertyType)
            If (type1.IsValueType OrElse (type1 Is GetType(String))) Then
                Me.WriteValue( _
                    IIf((Not info2 Is Nothing), info2.GetValue(o), _
                        info3.GetValue(o, Nothing)))
        ElseIf GetType(IEnumerable).IsAssignableFrom(type1) Then
            Me.Write("...")
        Else
            Me.Write("{ }")
        End If
    End If
Next
If flag1 Then
    Me.WriteLine
End If
If (Me.level < Me.depth) Then
    Dim info4 As MemberInfo
    For Each info4 In infoArray1
        Dim info5 As FieldInfo = TryCast(info4,FieldInfo)
        Dim info6 As PropertyInfo = TryCast(info4,PropertyInfo)
        If ((Not info5 Is Nothing) OrElse (Not info6 Is Nothing)) Then
            Dim type2 As Type = IIf((Not info5 Is Nothing), info5.FieldType, _
                                                    info6.PropertyType)
            If (Not type2.IsValueType AndAlso (Not type2 Is GetType(String))) Then
```

```
                    Dim obj2 As Object = IIf((Not info5 Is Nothing), info5.GetValue(o), _
                                                            info6.GetValue(o, Nothing))
                    If (Not obj2 Is Nothing) Then
                        Me.level += 1
                        Me.WriteObject((info4.Name & ": "), obj2)
                        Me.level -= 1
                    End If
                End If
            End If
        Next
    End If
    End If
End Sub
```

The Write method makes an internal call to the WriteObject private method that is the real core of all the ObjectDumper class. In the first section of the code it checks if the object is Nothing, a String, or an Object representing a value type. In the case of a value type, an output is provided without other checks. Instead, when the parameter Object o implements the IEnumerable(Of T) interface, the method code goes through each element of the parameter to check if other elements implement IEnumerable(Of T). If not, the object will be passed again to the same method, which will use .NET Reflection to get its value.

The query expression is evaluated in the For Each statement, where the query execution is really done.

It's possible to cache the result of a query using the ToList and ToArray methods. Let's look at the example in Listing 1-9:

Listing 1-9. The ToArray Method in Action

```
Dim people As List(Of Person) = New List(Of Person) { _
    {ID := 1, IDRole := 1, LastName := "Anderson", FirstName := "Brad"}, _
    {ID := 2, IDRole := 2, LastName := "Gray", FirstName := "Tom"} _
}

Dim query = (From p In people _
    Where p.ID = 1 _
    Select New {p.FirstName, p.LastName}).ToArray()

ObjectDumper.Write(query)

people(0).FirstName = "Fabio"

ObjectDumper.Write(query)
```

In Listing 1-9 the code caches the result of a query using the ToArray method. As the output in Figure 1-3 shows, even if the code changes an element of the List(Of T) collection, the query returns the same result since it has been cached.

Figure 1-3. The output of the ToArray example in Listing 1-9

Standard Query Operators

LINQ provides an API known as *standard query operators* (SQOs) to support the kinds of operations we're accustomed to in SQL. You've already used VB's Select and Where keywords, which map to LINQ's Select and Where SQOs—which, like all SQOs, are actually methods of the System.Query.Sequence shared class. Table 1-1 is a complete listing of SQOs.

Table 1-1. LINQ Standard Query Operators Grouped by Operation

Operation	Operator	Description
Aggregate	Aggregate	Applies a function over a sequence
--	Average	Calculates the average over a sequence
--	Count/LongCount	Counts the element of a sequence
--	Max	Returns the maximum value from a sequence of numeric values
--	Min	Returns the minimum value from a sequence of numeric values
--	Sum	Returns the sum of all numeric values from a sequence

(Continued)

Ferracchiati

Operation	Operator	Description
Concatenation	Concat	Merges elements from two sequences
Conversion	Cast	Casts an element of the sequence into a specified type
--	OfType	Filters elements of a sequence, returning only those of the specified type
--	ToArray	Converts the sequence into an array
--	ToDictionary	Creates a Dictionary(Of Tkey, Tvalue) from a sequence
--	ToList	Creates a List(Of T) from a sequence
--	ToLookup	Creates a Lookup(Of K,T) from a sequence
--	ToSequence	Returns its argument typed as Ienumerable(Of T)
Element	DefaultIfEmpty	Provides a default element for an empty sequence
--	ElementAt	Returns the element at the specified index from a sequence
--	ElementAtOrDefault	Similar to ElementAt but also returns a default element when the specified index is out of range
--	First	Returns the first element in a sequence
--	FirstOrDefault	Similar to First but also returns a default element when the first element in the sequence is not available

Operation	Operator	Description
--	Last	Returns the last element in a sequence
--	LastOrDefault	Similar to Last but also returns a default element when the last element in the sequence is not available
--	Single	Returns a sequence's single element that satisfies a condition specified as an argument
--	SingleOrDefault	Similar to Single but also returns a default value when the single element is not found in the sequence
Equality	EqualAll	Checks whether two sequences are equal
Generation	Empty	Returns an empty sequence for the specified data type
--	Range	Generates a numeric sequence from a range of two numbers
--	Repeat	Generates a sequence by repeating the provided element a specified number of times
Grouping	GroupBy	Groups the elements of a sequence
Join	GroupJoin	Performs a grouped join of two sequences based on matching keys
--	Join	Performs an inner join of two sequences based on matching keys

(Continued)

Operation	Operator	Description
Ordering	OrderBy	Orders the elements of the sequence according to one or more keys
--	OrderByDescending	Similar to OrderBy but sorts the sequence inversely
--	Reverse	Reverses the elements of the sequence
--	ThenBy	Useful for specifying additional ordering keys after the first one specified by either the OrderBy or OrderByDescending operator
--	ThenByDescending	Similar to ThenBy but sorts the sequence inversely
Partitioning	Skip	Skips a given number of elements from a sequence and then yields the remainder of the sequence
--	SkipWhile	Similar to Skip but the numbers of elements to skip are defined by a Boolean condition
--	Take	Takes a given number of elements from a sequence and skips the remainder of the sequence
--	TakeWhile	Similar to Take but the numbers of elements to take are defined by a Boolean condition
Projection	Select	Defines the elements to pick in a sequence
--	SelectMany	Performs a one-to-many-elements projection over a sequence

Operation	Operator	Description
Quantifier	All	Checks all the elements of a sequence against the provided condition
--	Any	Checks whether any element of the sequence satisfies the provided condition
--	Contains	Checks for an element's presence into a sequence
Restriction	Where	Filters a sequence based on the provided condition
Set	Distinct	Returns distinct elements from a sequence
--	Except	Produces a sequence that is the difference between elements of two sequences
--	Intersect	Produces a sequence resulting from the common elements of two sequences
--	Union	Produces a sequence that is the union of two sequences

In the rest of this chapter we'll examine each operator carefully, and consider examples that illustrate the elements' functionality. The examples will be based on numeric sequences for operators that use numbers, and on classes such as Person, Role, and Salary for operators that use more-complex sequences. Listing 1-10 shows these classes.

Listing 1-10. The Person, Role, and Salary classes

```
Public Class Person
    Dim _id As Integer
    Dim _idRole As Integer
    Dim _lastName As String
    Dim _firstName As String

    Public Property ID() As Integer
```

```vb
        Get
            Return _id
        End Get
        Set(ByVal value As Integer)
            _id = value
        End Set
    End Property

    Public Property IDRole() As Integer
        Get
            Return _idRole
        End Get
        Set(ByVal value As Integer)
            _idRole = value
        End Set
    End Property

    Public Property LastName() As String
        Get
            Return _lastName
        End Get
        Set(ByVal value As String)
            _lastName = value
        End Set
    End Property

    Public Property FirstName() As String
        Get
            Return _firstName
        End Get
        Set(ByVal value As String)
            _firstName = value
        End Set
    End Property

End Class

Public Class Role
    Dim _id As Integer
    Dim _roleDescription As String

    Public Property ID() As Integer
        Get
```

```vbnet
        Return _id
      End Get
      Set(ByVal value As Integer)
        _id = value
      End Set
    End Property

    Public Property RoleDescription() As String
      Get
        Return _roleDescription
      End Get
      Set(ByVal value As String)
        _roleDescription = value
      End Set
    End Property

End Class

Public Class Salary
    Dim _idPerson As Integer
    Dim _year As Integer
    Dim _salary As Double

    Public Property IDPerson() As Integer
      Get
        Return _idPerson
      End Get
      Set(ByVal value As Integer)
        _idPerson = value
      End Set
    End Property

    Public Property Year() As Integer
      Get
        Return _year
      End Get
      Set(ByVal value As Integer)
        _year = value
      End Set
    End Property

    Public Property SalaryYear() As Double
      Get
```

```
      Return _salary
    End Get
    Set(ByVal value As Double)
      _salary = value
    End Set
  End Property

End Class
```

The Person class provides four properties, one of which is the matching key with the second class, Role. The Role class provides two public properties to store the role identifier and its description. The Salary class provides the IDPerson foreign key to join to the Person class.

Let's now look at all the operators, starting with the most used ones.

Restriction Operator

There is one restriction operator: Where.

Where

One of the most used LINQ operators is Where. It restricts the sequence returned by a query based on a predicate provided as an argument.

```
<Extension> _
Public Shared Function Where(Of T)(ByVal source As IEnumerable(Of T), _
                                 ByVal predicate As Func(Of T, Boolean)) _
                                 As IEnumerable(Of T)

<Extension> _
Public Shared Function Where(Of T)(ByVal source As IEnumerable(Of T), _
                                 ByVal predicate As Func(Of T, Integer, Boolean)) _
                                 As IEnumerable(Of T)
```

The two forms differ in the second parameter, the predicate. It indicates the condition that has to be checked for each element of a sequence. The second form also accepts an int representing the zero-based index of the element of the source sequence.

Both operators extend the IEnumerable(Of T) type. Let's look at a couple of examples.

The code snippet in Listing 1-11 uses Where (through the VB Where keyword) to retrieve every element in a sequence that has FirstName equal to Brad. Figure 1-4 shows the output.

Listing 1-11. The Where Operator in Action

```
Dim people As List(Of Person) = New List(Of Person) { _
    {ID := 1, IDRole := 1, LastName := "Anderson", FirstName := "Brad"}, _
    {ID := 2, IDRole := 2, LastName := "Gray", FirstName := "Tom"} _
}

Dim query = From p In people _
    Where p.FirstName = "Brad" _
    Select p

ObjectDumper.Write(query)
```

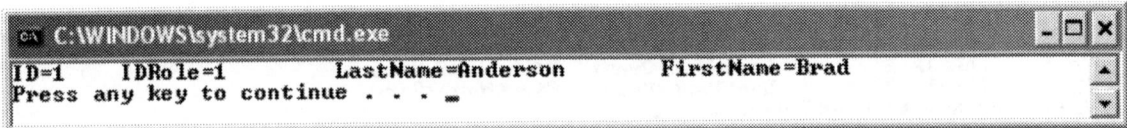

Figure 1-4. The output of Listing 1-11

Listing 1-12 uses the second Where form.

Listing 1-12. Using Where with an Index

```
Dim people As List(Of Person) = New List(Of Person) { _
    {ID := 1, IDRole := 1, LastName := "Anderson", FirstName := "Brad"}, _
    {ID := 2, IDRole := 2, LastName := "Gray", FirstName := "Tom"}, _
    {ID := 3, IDRole := 2, LastName := "Grant", FirstName := "Mary"}, _
    {ID := 4, IDRole := 3, LastName := "Cops", FirstName := "Gary"} _
}

Public Class WhereWithIndex
    Private Shared whereDelegate As Func(Of Person, Integer, Boolean)

    Private Shared Function whereCondition(ByVal p As Person, ByVal index As Integer) _
                            As Boolean
        Return (p.IDRole = index)
    End Function

    Public Sub Listing1_12(ByVal people As List(Of Person))
        whereDelegate = New Func(Of Person, Integer, Boolean)(AddressOf whereCondition)

        Dim result As IEnumerable(Of Person) = Sequence.Where(Of Person)(people, _
```

```
whereDelegate)
```

ObjectDumper.Write(result)

End Sub

End Class

In this case, the condition specified in the whereCondition function yields each sequence element whose index equals IDRole. The people data source shows that this is true only for the last element, as you can see in Figure 1-5.

```
C:\WINDOWS\system32\cmd.exe                                            _ □ ×
ID=3      IDRole=2        LastName=Grant   FirstName=Mary
ID=4      IDRole=3        LastName=Cops    FirstName=Gary
Press any key to continue . . . ▄
```

Figure 1-5. The output for the Where example in Listing 1-12

Projection Operators

There are two projection operators: Select and SelectMany.

Select

Just like SELECT in SQL, the Select operator specifies which elements are to be retrieved.

```
<Extension> _
Public Shared Function [Select](Of T, S)(ByVal source As IEnumerable(Of T), _
                                ByVal selector As Func(Of T, S)) _
                                As IEnumerable(Of S)

<Extension> _
Public Shared Function [Select](Of T, S)(ByVal source As IEnumerable(Of T), _
                                ByVal selector As Func(Of T, Integer, S)) _
                                As IEnumerable(Of S)
```

Both operators extend the IEnumerable(Of T) type. They differ in the second parameter. The first form accepts a selector function, where we can define the element to pick; the second also accepts a zero-based index indicating the position of the element in the sequence. Let's look at a couple of examples. The code snippet in Listing 1-13 returns all the elements from the sequence, just like SELECT * in SQL. Figure 1-6 shows the output.

Listing 1-13. Using the First Form of Select

```
Dim people As List(Of Person) = New List(Of Person) { _
    {ID := 1, IDRole := 1, LastName := "Anderson", FirstName := "Brad"}, _
    {ID := 2, IDRole := 2, LastName := "Gray", FirstName := "Tom"}, _
    {ID := 3, IDRole := 2, LastName := "Grant", FirstName := "Mary"}, _
    {ID := 4, IDRole := 3, LastName := "Cops", FirstName := "Gary"} _
}

Dim query = From p In people _
                    Select p

ObjectDumper.Write(query)
```

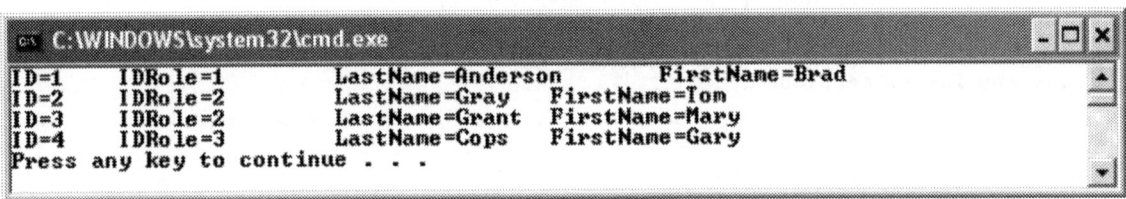

Figure 1-6. The output of Listing 1-13

Listing 1-14 uses an index to specify the element position in the sequence.

Listing 1-14. Using an Index with Select

```
Public Class SelectWithIndex
    Private Shared selectDelegate As Func(Of Person, Integer, Projection)

    Private Shared Function selectProjection(ByVal p As Person, _
                                        ByVal index As Integer) As Projection

        Dim proj As New Projection
        proj.Position = index
        proj.FirstName = p.FirstName
        proj.LastName = p.LastName

        Return proj
    End Function
```

```
Public Sub Listing1_13(ByVal people As List(Of Person))
    selectDelegate = New Func(Of Person, Integer, Projection)(AddressOf selectProjection)

    Dim result As IEnumerable(Of Projection) = _
                        Sequence.Select(Of Person, Projection)(people, selectDelegate)

    ObjectDumper.Write(result)

End Sub
End Class
```

This code snippet creates an anonymous type called Projection, formed by the full name of the person anticipated by the element position in the sequence. See Figure 1-7 for the output.

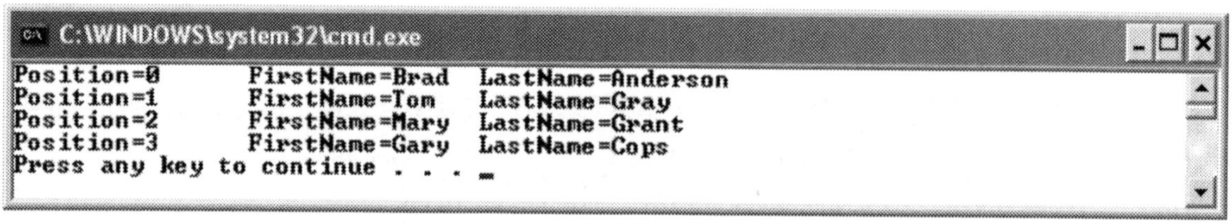

Figure 1-7. The output of Listing 1-14

SelectMany

This operator is similar to Select because it allows us to define the elements to pick from a sequence. The difference is in the return type.

```
<Extension> _
Public Shared Function SelectMany(Of T, S)(ByVal source As IEnumerable(Of T), _
ByVal selector As Func(Of T, IEnumerable(Of S))) As IEnumerable(Of S)

<Extension> _
Public Shared Function SelectMany(Of T, S)(ByVal source As IEnumerable(Of T), _
                              ByVal selector _
                              As Func(Of T, Integer, IEnumerable(Of S))) _
                              As IEnumerable(Of S)
```

With the IEnumerable(Of S) type returned by the selector parameter of SelectMany, it's possible to concatenate many projection operations together, either on different sequences or starting from the result of a previous query.

The SelectMany operator extends the IEnumerable(Of T) type. The selector parameter has two formats: the first returns the IEnumerable(Of S) type and the second also requires a zero-based index that specifies the position of the element in the sequence. Listings 1-14 and 1-15 clarify the differences between Select and SelectMany.

Listing 1-15. The SelectMany Method in Action

```
Dim people As List(Of Person) = New List(Of Person) { _
    {ID := 1, IDRole := 1, LastName := "Anderson", FirstName := "Brad"}, _
    {ID := 2, IDRole := 2, LastName := "Gray", FirstName := "Tom"}, _
    {ID := 3, IDRole := 2, LastName := "Grant", FirstName := "Mary"}, _
    {ID := 4, IDRole := 3, LastName := "Cops", FirstName := "Gary"} _
}

Dim roles As List(Of Role) = New List(Of Role) { _
    {ID := 1, RoleDescription := "Manager"}, _
    {ID := 2, RoleDescription := "Developer"} _
}

Dim query = From p In people, r In roles _
    Where p.ID = 1 AndAlso r.ID = p.IDRole _
    Select New {p.FirstName, p.LastName, r.RoleDescription}

ObjectDumper.Write(query)
```

This code snippet obtains a result similar to a database join, where the result of the first query is used in the other sequence to obtain the element corresponding to the match condition. Figure 1-8 shows the output.

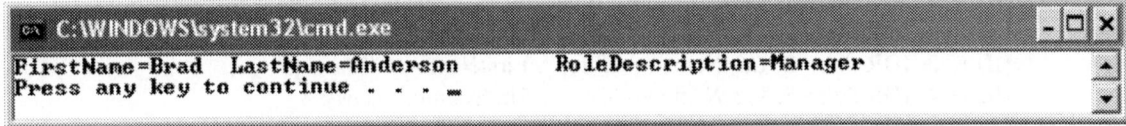

Figure 1-8. The output of Listing 1-15

SelectMany allows us to manage another sequence since it returns an IEnumerable(Of S), where S is the sequence. If we use the Select operator instead of SelectMany, we will get an IEnumerable(List(Of T)). This object is not composed of the sequence but of List(Of T) elements.

Join Operators

There are two join operators: Join and GroupJoin.

Join

Like INNER JOIN in SQL, the Join operator combines two sequences based on matching keys supplied as arguments. The Join operator is not overloaded.

```
<Extension> _
Public Shared Function Join(Of T, U, K, V)(ByVal outer As IEnumerable(Of T), _
                                ByVal inner As IEnumerable(Of U), _
                                ByVal outerKeySelector As Func(Of T, K), _
                                ByVal innerKeySelector As Func(Of U, K), _
                                ByVal resultSelector As Func(Of T, U, V)) _
                                As IEnumerable(Of V)
```

The Join operator extends the IEnumerable(Of T) type. The first parameter is one of the two sequences to join. It will be evaluated against the function specified as the outerKeySelector parameter. The second parameter contains the inner sequence used during the evaluation of the inner elements against the function specified as the innerKeySelector parameter. For each matching inner element the resultSelector function, specified as the last parameter, is evaluated for the outer and inner element pair, and the resulting object is returned. Listing 1-16 provides an example. Figure 1-9 shows the output. As you can see, only the Person records having a matching IDRole are displayed. The IDRole equal to 3 is excluded from the final result because it is not present in the roles list.

Listing 1-16. The Join Operator in Action

```
Dim people As List(Of Person) = New List(Of Person) { _
    {ID := 1, IDRole := 1, LastName := "Anderson", FirstName := "Brad"}, _
    {ID := 2, IDRole := 2, LastName := "Gray", FirstName := "Tom"}, _
    {ID := 3, IDRole := 2, LastName := "Grant", FirstName := "Mary"}, _
    {ID := 4, IDRole := 3, LastName := "Cops", FirstName := "Gary"} _
}

Dim roles As List(Of Role) = New List(Of Role) { _
    {ID := 1, RoleDescription := "Manager"}, _
    {ID := 2, RoleDescription := "Developer"} _
}

Public Class JoinExample
    Private Shared Function outerDelegate(ByVal p As Person) As Integer
        Return p.IDRole
    End Function

    Private Shared Function innerDelegate(ByVal r As Role) As Integer
```

```
        Return r.ID
    End Function

    Private Shared Function resultDelegate(ByVal p As Person, ByVal r As Role) As Person
        Return p
    End Function


    Public Sub Listing1_16(ByVal people As List(Of Person), ByVal roles As List(Of Role))
        Dim outerKeySelector As New Func(Of Person, Integer)(AddressOf outerDelegate)
        Dim innerKeySelector As New Func(Of Role, Integer)(AddressOf innerDelegate)
        Dim resultSelector As New Func(Of Person, Role, Person)(AddressOf resultDelegate)

        Dim result As IEnumerable(Of Person) = _
                Sequence.Join(Of Person, Role, Integer, Person) _
                    (people, roles, outerKeySelector, innerKeySelector, resultSelector)

        ObjectDumper.Write(result)
    End Sub

End Class
```

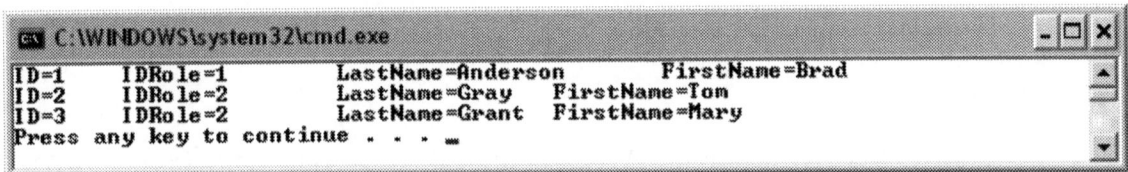

Figure 1-9. The output of Listing 1-16

GroupJoin

This operator is similar to Join but it returns the result in an IEnumerable(Of S) where S is a new sequence.

```
<Extension> _
Public Shared Function GroupJoin(Of T, U, K, V)(ByVal outer As IEnumerable(Of T), _
                                    ByVal inner As IEnumerable(Of U), _
                                    ByVal outerKeySelector As Func(Of T, K), _
                                    ByVal innerKeySelector As Func(Of U, K), _
                                    ByVal resultSelector As _
                                    Func(Of T, IEnumerable(Of U), V)) _
                                    As IEnumerable(Of V)
```

This operator is really useful when we have to implement particular joins, such as SQL's LEFT OUTER join. Listing 1-17 provides and example:

Listing 1-17. GroupJoin in Action

```
Dim people As List(Of Person) = New List(Of Person) { _
    {ID := 1, IDRole := 1, LastName := "Anderson", FirstName := "Brad"}, _
    {ID := 2, IDRole := 2, LastName := "Gray", FirstName := "Tom"}, _
    {ID := 3, IDRole := 2, LastName := "Grant", FirstName := "Mary"}, _
    {ID := 4, IDRole := 3, LastName := "Cops", FirstName := "Gary"} _
}

Dim roles As List(Of Role) = New List(Of Role) { _
    {ID := 1, RoleDescription := "Manager"}, _
    {ID := 2, RoleDescription := "Developer"} _
}

Public Class GroupJoinExample
    Private Shared Function outerDelegate(ByVal p As Person) As Integer
        Return p.IDRole
    End Function

    Private Shared Function innerDelegate(ByVal r As Role) As Integer
        Return r.ID
    End Function

    Private Shared Function resultDelegate(ByVal p As Person, ByVal pr As IEnumerable(Of Role)) As
IEnumerable(Of Role)
        Return pr
    End Function

    Public Sub Listing1_17(ByVal people As List(Of Person), ByVal roles As List(Of Role))
        Dim outerKeySelector As New Func(Of Person, Integer)(AddressOf outerDelegate)
        Dim innerKeySelector As New Func(Of Role, Integer)(AddressOf innerDelegate)
        Dim resultSelector As New Func(Of Person, IEnumerable(Of Role), _
IEnumerable(Of Role))(AddressOf resultDelegate)

        Dim result As IEnumerable(Of IEnumerable(Of Role)) = _
                Sequence.GroupJoin(Of Person, Role, Integer, IEnumerable(Of Role)) _
                    (people, roles, outerKeySelector, innerKeySelector, resultSelector)
        ObjectDumper.Write(result, 1)
    End Sub
```

In the code snippet in Listing 1-17 the GroupJoin standard query operator is used to group the join into a new sequence of Role elements called pr returned by the resultDelegate delegate function. The pr sequence will contain elements from the roles sequence that have matching IDRole and ID fields of the inputted people and roles sequences.See the output in Figure 1-10..

```
C:\WINDOWS\system32\cmd.exe                                    - □ ×
...
 ID=1       RoleDescription=Manager
...
 ID=2       RoleDescription=Developer
...
 ID=2       RoleDescription=Developer
...
Press any key to continue . . . _
```

Figure 1-10. The output of Listing 1-17

Grouping Operator

There is one grouping operator: GroupBy.

GroupBy

Just like the GROUP BY clause of SQL, the GroupBy operator groups elements of a sequence based on a given selector function.

```
<Extension> _
Public Shared Function GroupBy(Of T, K)(ByVal source As IEnumerable(Of T), _
ByVal keySelector As Func(Of T, K)) As IEnumerable(Of IGrouping(Of K, T))


<Extension> _
Public Shared Function GroupBy(Of T, K)(ByVal source As IEnumerable(Of T), _
                              ByVal keySelector As Func(Of T, K), _
                              ByVal comparer As IEqualityComparer(Of K)) _
                              As IEnumerable(Of IGrouping(Of K, T))


<Extension> _
Public Shared Function GroupBy(Of T, K, E)(ByVal source As IEnumerable(Of T), _
                              ByVal keySelector As Func(Of T, K), _
                              ByVal elementSelector As Func(Of T, E)) _
                              As IEnumerable(Of IGrouping(Of K, E))
```

```
<Extension> _
Public Shared Function GroupBy(Of T, K, E)(ByVal source As IEnumerable(Of T), _
                                ByVal keySelector As Func(Of T, K), _
                                ByVal elementSelector As Func(Of T, E), _
                                ByVal comparer As IEqualityComparer(Of K)) _
                                As IEnumerable(Of IGrouping(Of K, E))
```

Each GroupBy operator returns an IEnumerable(IGrouping(Of K, E)). Let's look at how IGrouping(Of K, T) is declared:

```
Public Interface IGrouping(Of K, T)
    Implements IEnumerable(Of T), IEnumerable

    ' Properties
    ReadOnly Property Key As K
End Interface
```

This interface implements IEnumerable(Of T) and adds a read-only property called Key. When the code process launches the query (that is when we are going to iterate through elements using a For Each statement) the source parameter is enumerated and evaluated against the keySelector and elementSelector functions (if specified). When every element has been evaluated and each element that satisfies the selector functions has been collected, new instances of the IGrouping(Of K, E) type are yielded. Finally, the IEqualityComparer interface, when specified, allows us to define a new way to compare elements of a sequence. Let's look at the example in Listing 1-18.

Listing 1-18. An Example of GroupBy Using .NET Reflection

```
Dim query = From m In GetType(Integer).GetMethods() _
    Select m.Name

ObjectDumper.Write(query)

Console.WriteLine("-=-=-=-=-=-=-=-=-=")
Console.WriteLine("After the GroupBy")
Console.WriteLine("-=-=-=-=-=-=-=-=-=")

Dim q = From m In GetType(Integer).GetMethods() _
    Group By m.Name _
    Select New {Name := it.Key}

ObjectDumper.Write(q)
```

The first query expression calls the GetMethods method provided by .NET Reflection to retrieve the list of available methods for the Integer type. Since GetMethods returns a MethodInfo() array, LINQ query expressions could use it easily too. The first part of the output shows the methods for the Integer type without the grouping (see Figure 1-11). The second part of the code snippet in Listing 1-18 uses the Group By clause to group the elements by method name. The result of the Group By clause is automatically inserted into the variable it of the new IGrouping(Of K, E) type that provides the Key property.

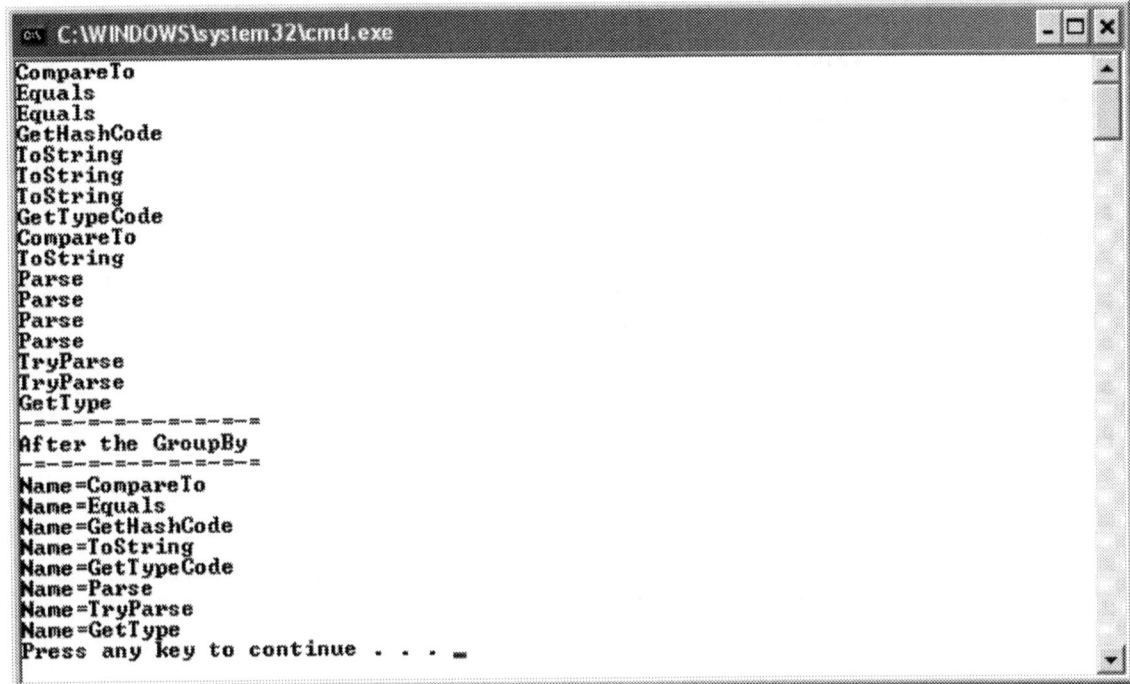

Figure 1-11. The output of Listing 1-18

In Listing 1-19 I added the Count operator to compute the number of method overloads.

Listing 1-19. Another Example of Group By Clause

```
Dim query = From m In GetType(Integer).GetMethods() _
    Group By m.Name _
    Select New {Name := it.Key, Overloads := it.Count}

ObjectDumper.Write(query)
```

The it variable represents the result of the Group By operation; it's possible to operate against this variable to filter its element, specify a Where clause, and so on. In this case the code snippet shows the result of counting the number of elements for each key in the group. In this case it represents the method's overloads. See Figure 1-12 for the output.

```
C:\WINDOWS\system32\cmd.exe                                         _ □ ×
Name=CompareTo    Overloads=2
Name=Equals       Overloads=2
Name=GetHashCode           Overloads=1
Name=ToString     Overloads=4
Name=GetTypeCode           Overloads=1
Name=Parse        Overloads=4
Name=TryParse     Overloads=2
Name=GetType      Overloads=1
Press any key to continue . . . _
```

Figure 1-12. The output of Listing 1-19

The last example for the grouping operator uses the comparer parameter, which allows us to customize the behavior of the Group By method during its work. See Listing 1-20.

Listing 1-20. The GroupBy Operator with a Custom Comparison Method

```
Public Class MyComparer
    Implements IEqualityComparer(Of String)

    ' Methods
    Public Function Equals(ByVal x As String, ByVal y As String) As Boolean Implements
System.Collections.Generic.IEqualityComparer(Of String).Equals
        Return (x.Substring(0, 2) = y.Substring(0, 2))
    End Function

    Public Function GetHashCode(ByVal obj As String) As Integer Implements
System.Collections.Generic.IEqualityComparer(Of String).GetHashCode
        Return obj.Substring(0, 2).GetHashCode
    End Function

End Class

    Dim dictionary As String() = New String() _
        {"F:Apple", "F:Banana", _
        "T:House", "T:Phone", _
        "F:Cherry", "T:Computer"}

    Dim comparerDelegate As New Func(Of String, String)(AddressOf comparer)
```

```
Dim query = Sequence.GroupBy(Of String, String)(dictionary, comparerDelegate, _
        New MyComparer)
```

```
ObjectDumper.Write(query, 1)
```

The dictionary array contains two kinds of objects. The F: prefix stands for *fruit* and the T: prefix stands for *thing*. We have defined a way to group fruit with fruit and thing with thing. To create a custom comparer we have to define a new class that implements the IEqualityComparer(Of T) interface. The contract subordinated by this interface forces us to implement two methods: Equals and GetHashCode. For Equals we have to insert the custom logic for our comparer. GetHashCode has to return the hash code for the same string checked in the Equals method. In Listing 1-20 we have a simple way to check the category of the strings. By analyzing their first two characters we know that F: stands for *fruit* and T: stands for *thing*. We simply have to check that both strings provided to the Equals method contain the same substring. Figure 1-13 shows the output for Listing 1-20.

Figure 1-13. We have grouped fruits and things.

Ordering Operators

There are five ordering operators: OrderBy, OrderByDescending, ThenBy, ThenByDescending, and Reverse.

OrderBy and OrderByDescending

Like ORDER BY and ORDER BY DESC in SQL, the OrderBy and OrderByDescending operators order elements of a sequence according to a given key. The OrderByDescending operator inverts the ordering.

```
<Extension> _
Public Shared Function OrderBy(Of T, K)(ByVal source As IEnumerable(Of T), _
```

```
                              ByVal keySelector As Func(Of T, K)) _
                              As OrderedSequence(Of T)


<Extension> _
Public Shared Function OrderBy(Of T, K)(ByVal source As IEnumerable(Of T), _
                              ByVal keySelector As Func(Of T, K), _
                              ByVal comparer As IComparer(Of K)) _
                              As OrderedSequence(Of T)


<Extension> _
Public Shared Function OrderByDescending(Of T, K) _
                    (ByVal source As IEnumerable(Of T), _
                     ByVal keySelector As Func(Of T, K)) _
                     As OrderedSequence(Of T)


<Extension> _
Public Shared Function OrderByDescending(Of T, K) _
                    (ByVal source As IEnumerable(Of T), _
                     ByVal keySelector As Func(Of T, K), _
                     ByVal comparer As IComparer(Of K)) _
                     As OrderedSequence(Of T)
```

The keySelector parameter is used to extract the elements from the sequence. When
specified the comparer parameter compares the elements. When the code processes the query,
the method collects all the elements and evaluates each of them against the keySelector.
Finally, an OrderedSequence(Of T) type is produced. This is similar to IEnumerable(Of T) except
that it doesn't provide public methods. Listing 1-21 provides an example.

Listing 1-21. This Code Snippet Adds the orderby Operator to the .NET Reflection Example

```
Dim query = From m In GetType(Integer).GetMethods() _
    Group By m.Name _
    Select New {Name := it.Key} _
    Order By Name


ObjectDumper.Write(query)
```

The code snippet in Listing 1-21 retrieves the Integer type's methods ordered by their
names. See Figure 1-14 for the output.

Figure 1-14. The output for Listing 1-21

To obtain descending order, you simply add the Descending keyword.

Order By m.Name Descending

ThenBy and ThenByDescending

As you saw in the previous section, Order By allows us to specify only one ordering key. We have to use either ThenBy or ThenByDescending to concatenate ordering-key values.

```
<Extension> _
Public Shared Function ThenBy(Of T, K)(ByVal source As OrderedSequence(Of T), _
                                ByVal keySelector As Func(Of T, K)) _
                                As OrderedSequence(Of T)


<Extension> _
Public Shared Function ThenBy(Of T, K)(ByVal source As OrderedSequence(Of T), _
                                ByVal keySelector As Func(Of T, K), _
                                ByVal comparer As IComparer(Of K)) _
                                As OrderedSequence(Of T)


<Extension> _
Public Shared Function ThenByDescending(Of T, K) _
                  (ByVal source As OrderedSequence(Of T), _
                   ByVal keySelector As Func(Of T, K)) _
                   As OrderedSequence(Of T)


<Extension> _
Public Shared Function ThenByDescending(Of T, K) _
                        (ByVal source As OrderedSequence(Of T), _
                        ByVal keySelector As Func(Of T, K), _
                        ByVal comparer As IComparer(Of K)) _
                        As OrderedSequence(Of T)
```

Just like in the OrderBy operators, the first argument is the source sequence whose elements are evaluated against the keySelector parameter. Listing 1-22 shows a more complete OrderBy/ThenBy example.

Listing 1-22. The OrderBy and ThenBy Operators

```
Dim people As List(Of Person) = New List(Of Person) { _
    {ID := 1, IDRole := 1, LastName := "Anderson", FirstName := "Brad"}, _
    {ID := 2, IDRole := 2, LastName := "Gray", FirstName := "Tom"}, _
    {ID := 3, IDRole := 2, LastName := "Grant", FirstName := "Mary"}, _
    {ID := 4, IDRole := 3, LastName := "Cops", FirstName := "Gary"} _
}

Dim query = From p In people _
    Select p _
    Order By p.FirstName, p.LastName

ObjectDumper.Write(query)
```

When the compiler encounters the query pattern in Listing 1-22 it transforms the first argument of the orderby operator to a call to the OrderBy() method, and transforms every other parameter after the comma to a related ThenBy() method call. Figure 1-15 shows the output of this code snippet.

```
C:\WINDOWS\system32\cmd.exe
ID=1      IDRole=1          LastName=Anderson          FirstName=Brad
ID=4      IDRole=3          LastName=Cops     FirstName=Gary
ID=3      IDRole=2          LastName=Grant    FirstName=Mary
ID=2      IDRole=2          LastName=Gray     FirstName=Tom
Press any key to continue . . .
```

Figure 1-15. The output of the ordered sequence shown in Listing 1-22

The last example of the ordering operators uses the comparer function (see Listing 1-23).

Listing 1-23. Using the comparer Function to Customize the Ordering Behavior

```
Public Class MyOrderingComparer
    Implements IComparer(Of String)

    Public Function Compare(ByVal x As String, ByVal y As String) As Integer _
            Implements System.Collections.Generic.IComparer(Of String).Compare
```

```
        x = x.Replace("_", String.Empty)
        y = y.Replace("_", String.Empty)
        Return String.Compare(x, y)

    End Function
End Class

Public Class OrderByWithComparer
    Private Shared Function comparer(ByVal w As String) As String
        Return w
    End Function

    Public Sub Listing1_23()
        Dim dictionary As String() = New String() {"Apple", "_Banana", "Cherry"}

        Dim comparerDelegate As New Func(Of String, String)(AddressOf comparer)

        Dim query = Sequence.OrderBy(Of String, String)(dictionary, comparerDelegate, _
                                        New MyOrderingComparer)

        ObjectDumper.Write(query)

    End Sub
End Class
```

To use the comparer parameter function we have to create a new class that implements the IComparer(Of T) interface. Its contract forces us to define the Compare() method, then add the comparing logic. In the code snippet in Listing 1-23 we want to treat the underscored string as a normal string when the ordering is implemented. So just before the Compare() method is called in the comparer function, we will remove each underscore from the source strings. See the output in Figure 1-16.

Figure 1-16. A custom comparer function allows us to change the ordering of the strings.

Reverse

This method simply returns a new sequence with elements in reverse ordering of the source sequence.

```
<Extension> _
Public Shared Function Reverse(Of T)(ByVal source As IEnumerable(Of T)) _
                                As IEnumerable(Of T)
```

When the code processes the query expression, the method enumerates the elements of the source sequence, collecting them in an IEnumerable(Of T) type. Before the method returns the result it inverts the ordering of the elements in the sequence.

Aggregate Operators

There are seven aggregate operators: Count, LongCount, Sum, Min, Max, Average, and Aggregate.

Count and LongCount

These methods return the number of elements within a sequence. The difference between them is in the return type. The Count method returns an integer and the LongCount method returns a long type. Let's see the methods' prototypes:

```
<Extension> _
Public Shared Function Count(Of T)(ByVal source As IEnumerable(Of T)) As Integer
```

```
<Extension> _
Public Shared Function Count(Of T)(ByVal source As IEnumerable(Of T), _
                                ByVal predicate As Func(Of T, Boolean)) As Integer
```

```
<Extension> _
Public Shared Function LongCount(Of T)(ByVal source As IEnumerable(Of T)) As Long
```

```
<Extension> _
Public Shared Function LongCount(Of T)(ByVal source As IEnumerable(Of T), _
ByVal predicate As Func(Of T, Boolean)) As Long
```

Both methods have two different prototypes. The former, without the predicate parameter, checks the type of the source parameter. If it implements the ICollection(Of T) type then its Count method is used. If it doesn't, the source sequence is enumerated, incrementing a number that represents the final count value. The latter uses the predicate function parameter, returning the count of elements against which the specified condition is true.

We have already used the Count operator in the "Grouping Operator" section; see Listing 1-19 for an example of the Count operator.

Sum

The Sum method computes the sum of numeric values within a sequence.

```
<Extension> _
Public Shared Function Sum(ByVal source As IEnumerable(Of Numeric)) As Numeric

<Extension> _
Public Shared Function Sum(Of T)(ByVal source As IEnumerable(Of T), _
                        ByVal selector As Func(Of T, Integer)) As Integer
```

The Numeric type returned from the Sum() method must be one of the following: Integer, Nullable(Of Integer), Int64, Nullable(Of Int64), Double, Nullable(Double), Decimal, or Nullable(Decimal).

Note ➡ The Nullable type specifies that a variable of that type can contain Nothing values. This feature was added to .NET 2.0 to provide greater compatibility with NULLABLE columns in database tables.

The first prototype without the selector parameter computes the sum of the elements in the sequence. When the selector parameter is used it picks the specified element of the sequence on which computing the sum will start. The Sum operator does not include Nothing values in the result, which means a zero will be returned for an empty sequence (see Listing 1-24).

Listing 1-24. A Code Snippet for the Sum Operator

```
Dim numbers As New Integer() {1, 2, 3, 4, 5, 6, 7, 8, 9}
Dim query As Integer = numbers.Sum()
ObjectDumper.Write(query)
```

The output for the code snippet in Listing 1-24 will be the sum of all the elements in the sequence: 45.

Another great use for the Sum operator is to have it work with the GroupBy operator to obtain total salary amounts, like the one shown in Listing 1-25.

Listing 1-25. Using Sum and GroupBy Operators to Obtain Salary Results

```
Dim salaries As New List(Of Salary) { _
        {IDPerson := 1, Year := 2004, SalaryYear := 10000.0}, _
        {IDPerson := 1, Year := 2005, SalaryYear := 15000.0}, _
        {IDPerson := 2, Year := 2005, SalaryYear := 15000.0} _
    }

Public Class SumExample
    Private Shared Function sumDelegate(ByVal s As Salary) As Double
        Return s.SalaryYear
    End Function

    Public Sub Listing1_25(ByVal salaries As List(Of Salary))
        Dim query = From s In salaries _
            Group By s.Year _
            Select it

        For Each Dim item In query
            Console.WriteLine("Year {0}: {1}", item.Key, _
                                        Sequence.Sum(Of Salary)(item, _
                                        New Func(Of Salary, Double)( _
                                                AddressOf sumDelegate)))

        Next
    End Sub

End Class
```

The salaries collection contains the total salary per year. We want to retrieve the total of salaries per year so the query groups records by the Year field, putting the result in the variable it. Next, the For Each loop goes through the elements of the query, calling the Sum(Of T) standard operator to compute the sum of the grouped salaries.

See Figure 1-17 for the output.

```
C:\WINDOWS\system32\cmd.exe                                                    _ □ ×
Year 2004: 10000
Year 2005: 30000
Press any key to continue . . .
```

Figure 1-17. The output for Listing 1-25

Min and Max

The Min and Max methods return the minimum and the maximum element within a sequence, respectively.

```
<Extension> _
Public Shared Function Min(ByVal source As IEnumerable(Of Numeric)) As Numeric


<Extension> _
Public Shared Function Min(Of T)(ByVal source As IEnumerable(Of T)) As T


<Extension> _
Public Shared Function Min(Of T)(ByVal source As IEnumerable(Of T), _
                        ByVal selector As Func(Of T, Numeric)) As Numeric


<Extension> _
Public Shared Function Min(Of T, S)(ByVal source As IEnumerable(Of T), _
                        ByVal selector As Func(Of T, S)) As S
<Extension> _
Public Shared Function Min(ByVal source As IEnumerable(Of Numeric)) As Numeric


<Extension> _
Public Shared Function Min(Of T)(ByVal source As IEnumerable(Of T)) As T


<Extension> _
Public Shared Function Min(Of T)(ByVal source As IEnumerable(Of T), _
                        ByVal selector As Func(Of T, Numeric)) As Numeric


<Extension> _
Public Shared Function Min(Of T, S)(ByVal source As IEnumerable(Of T), _
                        ByVal selector As Func(Of T, S)) As S
```

When the code processes the query expression, the Min and Max operators enumerate the source sequence and call the selector for each element, finding the minimum and maximum. When no selector function is specified, the minimum and the maximum are calculated by elements themselves.

Listing 1-26 shows retrieval of the minimum and the maximum salary for the Brad Anders person element.

Listing 1-26. Using the Min and Max Operators to Retrieve the Minimum and Maximum Salary

```
Dim people As List(Of Person) = New List(Of Person) { _
    {ID := 1, IDRole := 1, LastName := "Anderson", FirstName := "Brad"}, _
```

```
            {ID := 2, IDRole := 2, LastName := "Gray", FirstName := "Tom"}, _
            {ID := 3, IDRole := 2, LastName := "Grant", FirstName := "Mary"}, _
            {ID := 4, IDRole := 3, LastName := "Cops", FirstName := "Gary"} _
        }

    Dim salaries As New List(Of Salary) { _
            {IDPerson := 1, Year := 2004, SalaryYear := 10000.0}, _
            {IDPerson := 1, Year := 2005, SalaryYear := 15000.0}, _
            {IDPerson := 2, Year := 2005, SalaryYear := 15000.0} _
        }

    Dim query = From p In people, s In salaries _
        Where p.ID = 1 _
        Select s.SalaryYear

    Console.WriteLine("Minimum Salary:")
    Console.WriteLine(query.Min())

    Console.WriteLine("Maximum Salary:")
    Console.WriteLine(query.Max())
```

From the query expression we retrieve the salaries for the person that has the identifier equal to 1 and then we apply the Min and Max operators to the result. See Figure 1-18 for the output.

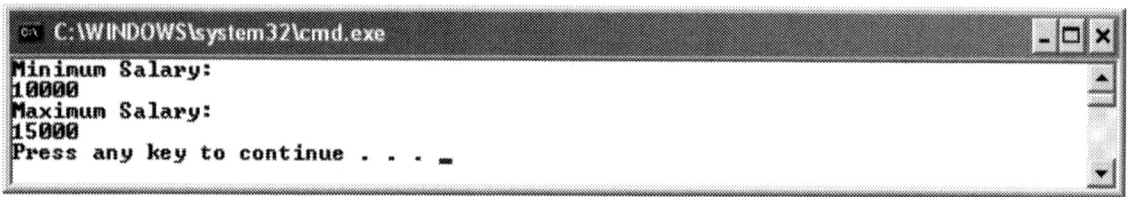

Figure 1-18. The Min and Max operators prompting the minimum and maximum salary

Average

This operator computes the average of the elements within a sequence.

```
<Extension> _
Public Shared Function Average(ByVal source As IEnumerable(Of Numeric)) As Numeric

<Extension> _
Public Shared Function Average(Of T)(ByVal source As IEnumerable(Of T), _
```

ByVal selector As Func(Of T, Decimal)) As Decimal

The Result type returned from the preceding prototypes will be either a Double or Nullable(Of Double) type when the Numeric type is Integer and Int64, or Nullable(Integer) and Nullable(Int64), respectively. When the Numeric type assumes other types, those will be returned as is.

When the average is computed, if the sum of the elements is too large to be contained in the Numeric type an overflow exception will be thrown. Listing 1-27 shows the operator in action.

Listing 1-27. Using the Average Operator to Compute the Average of the Salary

```
Dim people As List(Of Person) = New List(Of Person) { _
    {ID := 1, IDRole := 1, LastName := "Anderson", FirstName := "Brad"}, _
    {ID := 2, IDRole := 2, LastName := "Gray", FirstName := "Tom"}, _
    {ID := 3, IDRole := 2, LastName := "Grant", FirstName := "Mary"}, _
    {ID := 4, IDRole := 3, LastName := "Cops", FirstName := "Gary"} _
}

Dim salaries As New List(Of Salary) { _
    {IDPerson := 1, Year := 2004, SalaryYear := 10000.0}, _
    {IDPerson := 1, Year := 2005, SalaryYear := 15000.0}, _
    {IDPerson := 2, Year := 2005, SalaryYear := 15000.0} _
}

Dim query = From p In people, s In salaries _
    Where p.ID = 1 AndAlso p.ID = s.IDPerson _
    Select s.SalaryYear

Console.WriteLine("Average Salary:")
Console.WriteLine(query.Average())
```

From the query expression we retrieve the salaries for the person that has the identifier equal to 1 and then we apply the Average method to the result. See Figure 1-19 for the output.

Figure 1-19. The output for Listing 1-27

Aggregate

This operator allows us to define a function used during the aggregation of the elements in a sequence.

```
<Extension> _
Public Shared Function Aggregate(Of T)(ByVal source As IEnumerable(Of T), _
ByVal func As Func(Of T, T, T)) As T

<Extension> _
Public Shared Function Aggregate(Of T, U)(ByVal source As IEnumerable(Of T), _
                            ByVal seed As U, ByVal func As Func(Of U, T, U)) As U
```

The difference between those two prototypes stands in the seed parameter. When the seed parameter is not specified the method uses the specified function to aggregate the elements of the sequence, assuming the first element as seed. When seed is specified the operator uses the seed value as a starting point for applying the aggregate function. Let's look at an example in Listing 1-28:

Listing 1-28. The Aggregate Method in Action

```
Public Class AggregateExample
    Private Shared Function aggregateFunc(ByVal a As Integer, ByVal b As Integer) As Integer
        Return (a * b)
    End Function

    Public Sub Listing1_28()
        Dim numbers As Integer() = New Integer() {1, 2, 3, 4, 5, 6, 7, 8, 9}
        Dim aggregateDelegate As New Func(Of Integer, Integer, Integer) _
                                    (AddressOf aggregateFunc)
        Dim query = numbers.Aggregate(Of Integer)(aggregateDelegate)
        ObjectDumper.Write(query)
    End Sub
End Class
```

This code snippet uses the method without the seed parameter, so it takes the first element, 1, as seed, multiplying it for each other element in the sequence. The final result will be 362880.

In Listing 1-29 we will use the seed parameter.

Listing 1-29. The Aggregate Method Used with the seed Parameter

```
Public Class AggregateExampleWithSeed
    Private Shared Function aggregateFunc(ByVal a As Integer, ByVal b As Integer) As Integer
```

```
        Return IIf((a < b), (a * b), a)
    End Function


    Public Sub Listing1_29()
        Dim numbers As Integer() = New Integer() {9, 3, 5, 4, 2, 6, 7, 1, 8}
        Dim aggregateDelegate As New Func(Of Integer, Integer, Integer)(AddressOf aggregateFunc)
        Dim query = numbers.Aggregate(Of Integer, Integer)(5, aggregateDelegate)
        ObjectDumper.Write(query)
    End Sub
End Class
```

The method starts evaluating 5 with the first element in the sequence, 9. Since we have defined a rule where the element in the sequence is multiplied by the seed only if it is greater than the aggregated value, the method multiplies those two values, producing 45. This new value will be greater than any of the other elements in the sequence, so the final result will be 45.

Partitioning Operators

There are four partitioning operators: Take, Skip, TakeWhile, and SkipWhile.

Take

The Take method returns a given number of elements within a sequence and ignores the rest.

```
<Extension> _
Public Shared Function Take(Of T)(ByVal source As IEnumerable(Of T), _
                            ByVal count As Integer) As IEnumerable(Of T)
```

When the code processes the query expression, the source sequence is enumerated. This yields elements until the count parameter value is reached.

The Take and Skip methods are really useful when you need to implement a pagination-record mechanism. Listing 1-30 shows an easy approach to the pagination of elements within a sequence.

Listing 1-30. Take and Skip Methods to Reproduce a Pagination Mechanism

```
Dim numbers As Integer() = New Integer() {1, 2, 3, 4, 5, 6, 7, 8, 9}
Dim query = numbers.Take(5)
ObjectDumper.Write(query)
```

```
Console.Write("Press Enter key to see the other elements...")
Console.ReadLine()
Dim query2 = numbers.Skip(5)
ObjectDumper.Write(query2)
```

The first query yields just the first five elements of the sequence. After the Enter key is pressed another query is called, in which the Skip method ignores the first five elements, prompting the rest (see Figure 1-20).

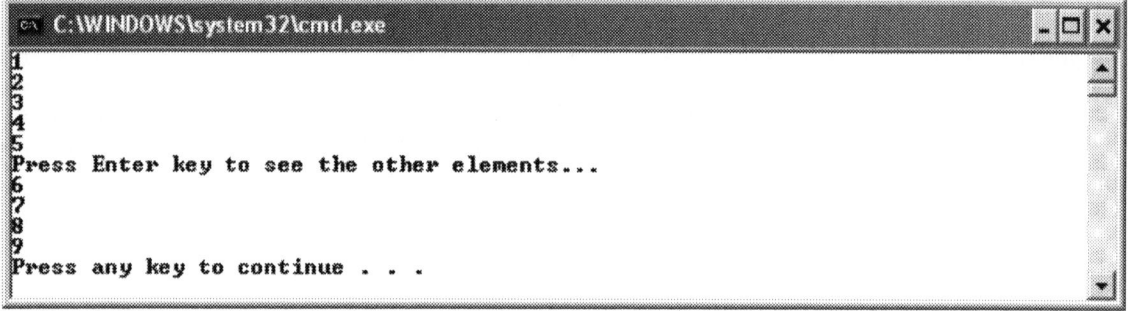

Figure 1-20. The output for Listing 1-30

Skip

This method skips a given number of elements within a sequence, yielding the rest.

```
<Extension> _
Public Shared Function Skip(Of T)(ByVal source As IEnumerable(Of T), _
                                  ByVal count As Integer) As IEnumerable(Of T)
```

When the code processes the query expression the source sequence is enumerated, skipping elements until the count parameter value is reached.

See Listing 1-30 and Figure 1-20 for a Skip-method example.

TakeWhile

This method returns the elements from a sequence while the predicate function specified is true.

```
<Extension> _
Public Shared Function TakeWhile(Of T)(ByVal source As IEnumerable(Of T), _
                                       ByVal predicate As Func(Of T, Boolean)) _
                                       As IEnumerable(Of T)
```

```
<Extension> _
Public Shared Function TakeWhile(Of T)(ByVal source As IEnumerable(Of T), _
                                ByVal predicate As Func(Of T, Integer, Boolean)) _
                                As IEnumerable(Of T)
```

When the code processes the query expression the source sequence is enumerated, testing each element against the predicate function. Each element that satisfies the condition is yielded. The second prototype provides a zero-based index related to the elements of the sequence.

Listing 1-31 provides an example of the TakeWhile and SkipWhile methods.

Listing 1-31. The TakeWhile and SkipWhile Methods in Action

```
Public Class TakeWhileExample
    Private Shared Function takeFunc(ByVal n As Integer, ByVal index As Integer) As Boolean
        Return (n >= index)
    End Function

    Private Shared Function skipFunc(ByVal n As Integer, ByVal index As Integer) As Boolean
        Return (n >= index)
    End Function


    Public Sub Listing1_31()
        Dim numbers As Integer() = New Integer() {9, 3, 5, 4, 2, 6, 7, 1, 8}
        Dim takeDelegate As New Func(Of Integer, Integer, Boolean)(AddressOf takeFunc)
        Dim skipDelegate As New Func(Of Integer, Integer, Boolean)(AddressOf skipFunc)
        Dim query = numbers.TakeWhile(takeDelegate)
        ObjectDumper.Write(query)
        Console.Write("Press Enter key to see the other elements...")
        Console.ReadLine()
        Dim query2 = numbers.SkipWhile(skipDelegate)
        ObjectDumper.Write(query2)
    End Sub
End Class
```

This code snippet uses the second TakeWhile prototype, where the index of the elements of the sequence acts as a condition of the predicate function. Until the element's index is less than or equal to its own value, it is yielded. The rest of the elements will be skipped. After the Enter key is pressed the SkipWhile method is used with the same predicate condition to yield the other elements. See Figure 1-21 for the resulting output.

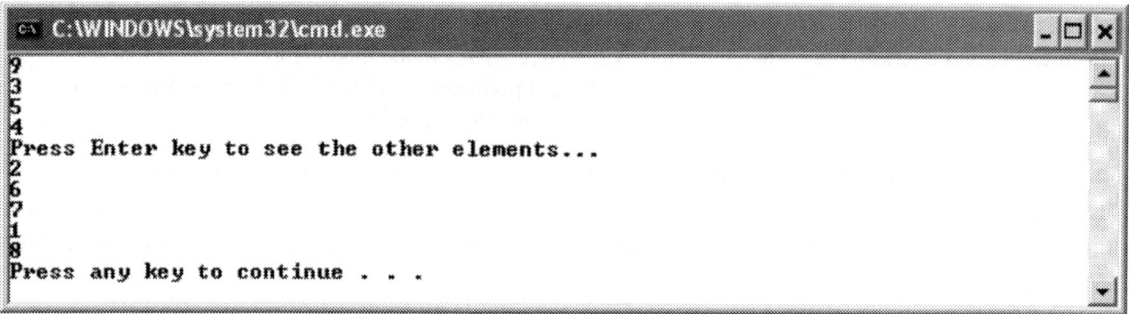

Figure 1-21. The output for Listing 1-31

SkipWhile

The SkipWhile operator skips elements from a sequence while the predicate function returns true, then it yields the rest.

```
<Extension> _
Public Shared Function SkipWhile(Of T)(ByVal source As IEnumerable(Of T), _
                                       ByVal predicate As Func(Of T, Boolean)) _
                                       As IEnumerable(Of T)


<Extension> _
Public Shared Function SkipWhile(Of T)(ByVal source As IEnumerable(Of T), _
                                       ByVal predicate As Func(Of T, Integer, Boolean)) _
                                       As IEnumerable(Of T)
```

Each source element is tested against the predicate function parameter. The element will be skipped if the predicate function returns True. The second prototype provides a zero-based index related to the elements of the sequence.

For an example of the SkipWhile method see Listing 1-31.

Concatenation Operator

There is one concatenation operator: Concat.

Concat

This operator concatenates two sequences.

```
<Extension> _
```

```
Public Shared Function Concat(Of T)(ByVal first As IEnumerable(Of T), _
                              ByVal second As IEnumerable(Of T)) _
                              As IEnumerable(Of T)
```

The resulting IEnumerable(Of T) type is the concatenation of the first and second sequences specified as a parameter.

In Listing 1-32 two numeric sequences are concatenated.

Listing 1-32. The Concat Method Used to Concatenate Two Numeric Sequences

```
Dim numbers As Integer() = New Integer() {1, 2, 3, 4, 5, 6, 7, 8, 9}
Dim moreNumbers As Integer() = New Integer() {10, 11, 12, 13}
Dim query = numbers.Concat(moreNumbers)
ObjectDumper.Write(query)
```

Starting from the numbers sequence the Concat method appends the moreNumbers sequence (see Figure 1-22).

Figure 1-22. The output of Listing 1-32

Element Operators

There are nine element operators: First, FirstOrDefault, Last, LastOrDefault, Single, SingleOrDefault, ElementAt, ElementAtOrDefault, and DefaultIfEmpty.

First, Last, FirstOrDefault, and LastOrDefault

These operators return the first/last element from a sequence.

```
<Extension> _
```

```
Public Shared Function First(Of T)(ByVal source As IEnumerable(Of T)) As T

<Extension> _
Public Shared Function First(Of T)(ByVal source As IEnumerable(Of T), ByVal predicate As Func(Of
T, Boolean)) As T

<Extension> _
Public Shared Function FirstOrDefault(Of T)(ByVal source As IEnumerable(Of T)) As T

<Extension> _
Public Shared Function FirstOrDefault(Of T)(ByVal source As IEnumerable(Of T), ByVal predicate As
Func(Of T, Boolean)) As T

<Extension> _
Public Shared Function Last(Of T)(ByVal source As IEnumerable(Of T)) As T

<Extension> _
Public Shared Function Last(Of T)(ByVal source As IEnumerable(Of T), ByVal predicate As Func(Of
T, Boolean)) As T

<Extension> _
Public Shared Function LastOrDefault(Of T)(ByVal source As IEnumerable(Of T)) As T

<Extension> _
Public Shared Function LastOrDefault(Of T)(ByVal source As IEnumerable(Of T), _
                                           ByVal predicate As Func(Of T, Boolean)) As T
```

When the predicate function parameter is specified, the method returns the first/last element against which the predicate function is satisfied, and therefore returns true. Otherwise the method returns simply the first/last element in the sequence. Listing 1-33 provides some examples.

Listing 1-33. Examples of the First and Last Methods

```
Public Class FirstLastExample
    Private Shared Function firstFunc(ByVal n As Integer) As Boolean
        Return (n Mod 2 = 0)
    End Function

    Private Shared Function lastFunc(ByVal n As Integer) As Boolean
        Return (n Mod 2 = 0)
    End Function
```

```
Public Sub Listing1_33()
    Dim numbers As Integer() = New Integer() {1, 2, 3, 4, 5, 6, 7, 8, 9}
    Dim firstDelegate As New Func(Of Integer, Boolean)(AddressOf firstFunc)
    Dim lastDelegate As New Func(Of Integer, Boolean)(AddressOf lastFunc)

    Dim query = numbers.First()
    Console.WriteLine("The first element in the sequence")
    ObjectDumper.Write(query)
    query = numbers.Last()
    Console.WriteLine("The last element in the sequence")
    ObjectDumper.Write(query)
    Console.WriteLine("The first even element in the sequence")
    query = numbers.First(firstDelegate)
    ObjectDumper.Write(query)
    Console.WriteLine("The last even element in the sequence")
    query = numbers.Last(lastDelegate)
    ObjectDumper.Write(query)
End Sub
End Class
```

In Listing 1-33 the First and Last methods are used to retrieve the first and last element of the numeric sequence, respectively. Moreover, when the predicate function is specified the First and Last methods return the first and last even element, respectively (see Figure 1-23).

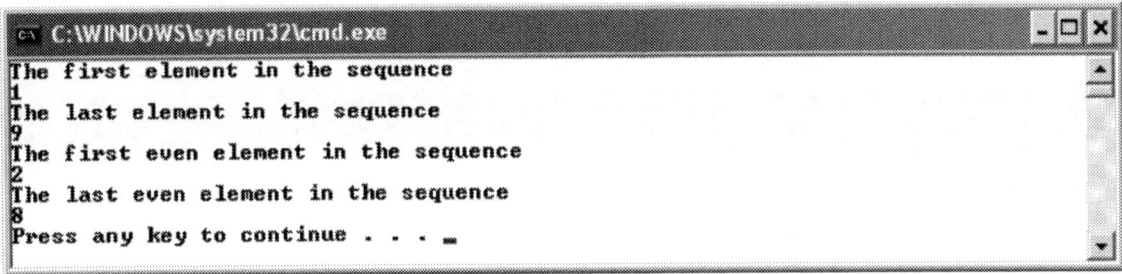

Figure 1-23. Sample output of the First and Last methods

Using the FirstOrDefault/LastOrDefault methods we would have obtained the same results. However, when we use those methods and a predicate does not find an element satisfying the specified condition, a default value is returned (thereby avoiding retrieval of an exception). See the example in Listing 1-34.

Ferracchiati

Listing 1-34. A FirstOrDefault/LastOrDefault Example

```
Public Class FirstLastOrDefaultExample
    Private Shared Function firstFunc(ByVal n As Integer) As Boolean
        Return (n Mod 2 = 0)
    End Function

    Private Shared Function lastFunc(ByVal n As Integer) As Boolean
        Return (n Mod 2 = 1)
    End Function


    Public Sub Listing1_34()
        Dim numbers As Integer() = New Integer() {1, 3, 5, 7, 9}
        Dim firstDelegate As New Func(Of Integer, Boolean)(AddressOf firstFunc)
        Dim lastDelegate As New Func(Of Integer, Boolean)(AddressOf lastFunc)

        Dim query = numbers.FirstOrDefault(firstDelegate)
        Console.WriteLine("The first even element in the sequence")
        ObjectDumper.Write(query)
        Console.WriteLine("The last odd element in the sequence")
        query = numbers.LastOrDefault(lastDelegate)
        ObjectDumper.Write(query)
    End Sub
End Class
```

Since no even numbers are in the sequence, FirstOrDefault returns the zero default value. On the other hand, the LastOrDefault operator looks for the last odd number in the sequence and finds the number 9. Figure 1-24 shows the output.

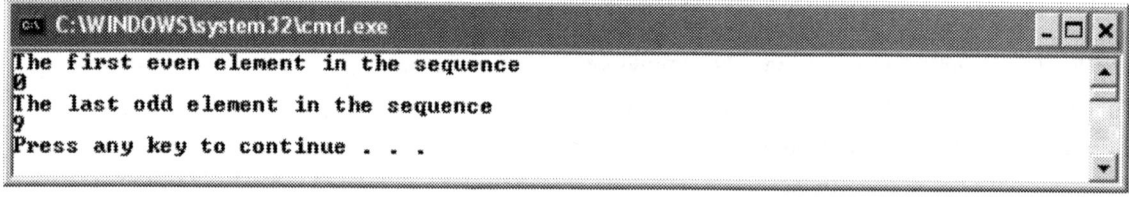

Figure 1-24. The output for Listing 1-34

Single and SingleOrDefault

These methods return a single element picked from a sequence.

```
<Extension> _
Public Shared Function [Single](Of T)(ByVal source As IEnumerable(Of T)) As T
```

```
<Extension> _
Public Shared Function [Single](Of T)(ByVal source As IEnumerable(Of T), _
                              ByVal predicate As Func(Of T, Boolean)) As T


<Extension> _
Public Shared Function SingleOrDefault(Of T)(ByVal source As IEnumerable(Of T)) As T


<Extension> _
Public Shared Function SingleOrDefault(Of T)(ByVal source As IEnumerable(Of T), _
                              ByVal predicate As Func(Of T, Boolean)) As T
```

When the predicate function is specified it will be used against each element until the function returns True. The element that satisfies the predicate will be returned. If more than one element satisfies the predicate function, an exception will be thrown. In Listing 1-35 just one element (9) satisfies the predicate condition that the elements must be greater than 8.

Listing 1-35. An Example of Single with a Predicate Condition

```
Public Class SingleExample
    Private Shared Function singleFunc(ByVal n As Integer) As Boolean
        Return (n > 8)
    End Function

    Public Sub Listing1_35()
        Dim numbers As Integer() = New Integer() {1, 3, 5, 7, 9}
        Dim singleDelegate As New Func(Of Integer, Boolean)(AddressOf singleFunc)

        Dim query = numbers.Single(singleDelegate)
        ObjectDumper.Write(query)
    End Sub
End Class
```

Using the Single method, if no element satisfies the predicate condition, an exception is thrown. Using the SingleOrDefault method (see Listing 1-36) either a Nothing or Zero value is returned when no element satisfies the predicate function. The difference between the Nothing and Zero value depends on the source type: Nothing for reference types (i.e., Strings) and Zero for value types (i.e., Integers).

Listing 1-36. The SingleOrDefault Method in Action

```
Public Class SingleOrDefaultExample
    Private Shared Function singleFunc(ByVal n As Integer) As Boolean
        Return (n > 9)
    End Function

    Public Sub Listing1_36()
        Dim numbers As Integer() = New Integer() {1, 3, 5, 7, 9}
        Dim singleDelegate As New Func(Of Integer, Boolean)(AddressOf singleFunc)

        Dim query = numbers.SingleOrDefault(singleDelegate)
        ObjectDumper.Write(query)
    End Sub
End Class
```

Since no numeric element is greater than 9, a Zero value will be returned.

ElementAt and ElementAtOrDefault

These methods return an element from the sequence at the specified zero-based index.

```
<Extension> _
Public Shared Function ElementAt(Of T)(ByVal source As IEnumerable(Of T), _
                                        ByVal index As Integer) As T

<Extension> _
Public Shared Function ElementAtOrDefault(Of T)(ByVal source As IEnumerable(Of T), _
                                        ByVal index As Integer) As T
```

When the code processes the query expression the method checks if the sequence implements the IList(Of T) type. If so the method uses the IList(Of T) implementation to obtain the element; otherwise the sequence will be enumerated until the index is reached.

Listing 1-37 uses ElementAt to retrieve the number 5 from the sequence.

Listing 1-37. Using ElementAt to Retrieve the Fifth Element

```
Dim numbers As Integer() = New Integer() {1, 2, 3, 4, 5, 6, 7, 8, 9}
Dim query = numbers.ElementAt(4)
ObjectDumper.Write(query)
```

When an invalid index is specified (i.e., an index less than zero) an exception of type ArgumentNullException is thrown. On the other hand, when using the ElementAtOrDefault method either a Nothing or Zero value will be returned (see Listing 1-38).

Listing 1-38. ElementAtOrDefault in Action

```
Dim numbers As Integer() = New Integer() {1, 2, 3, 4, 5, 6, 7, 8, 9}
Dim query = numbers.ElementAtOrDefault(9)
ObjectDumper.Write(query)
```

Since the tenth element is out of range the zero default value is returned.

DefaultIfEmpty

This operator replaces an empty element with a default element in a sequence, as in the following examples.

```
<Extension> _
Public Shared Function DefaultIfEmpty(Of T)(ByVal source As IEnumerable(Of T)) _
As IEnumerable(Of T)
```

```
<Extension> _
Public Shared Function DefaultIfEmpty(Of T)(ByVal source As IEnumerable(Of T), _
                                ByVal defaultValue As T) As IEnumerable(Of T)
```

If no default value parameter is specified, a Nothing element will be yielded. This method is useful to produce left outer joins.

Generation Operators

There are three generation operators: Empty, Range, and Repeat.

Empty

This operator returns an empty sequence of the specified type.

```
Public Shared Function Empty(Of T)() As IEnumerable(Of T)
```

When the IEnumerable(Of T) returned by the Empty(Of T) method is enumerated it yields nothing. Listing 1-39 shows how to produce an empty Person sequence:

Listing 1-39. An Empty Person Sequence Produced by the Empty(Of T) Method

```
Dim p As IEnumerable(Of Person) = Sequence.Empty(Of Person)()
ObjectDumper.Write(p)
```

The p variable contains no values, so the Write() method will not prompt any information.

Range

This operator produces a range of numeric values.

```
Public Shared Function Range(ByVal start As Integer, ByVal count As Integer) _
                                               As IEnumerable(Of Integer)
```

When the IEnumerable(Of Integer) type is enumerated it produces a sequence of count elements starting from the start parameter value. In Listing 1-40 a sequence of ten numbers will be generated.

Listing 1-40. A Numeric Sequence from 1 to 10 Is Generated

```
ObjectDumper.Write(Sequence.Range(1, 10))
```

Repeat

This operator produces a sequence by repeating a value a given number of times.

```
Public Shared Function Repeat(Of T)(ByVal element As T, ByVal count As Integer) _
                                               As IEnumerable(Of T)
```

The T element parameter will be generated the number of times indicated by the count parameter. In Listing 1-41 the first element of the Person sequence (people) is displayed ten times.

Listing 1-41. The Repeat Method in Action

```
Dim people As List(Of Person) = New List(Of Person) { _
    {ID := 1, IDRole := 1, LastName := "Anderson", FirstName := "Brad"}, _
    {ID := 2, IDRole := 2, LastName := "Gray", FirstName := "Tom"}, _
    {ID := 3, IDRole := 2, LastName := "Grant", FirstName := "Mary"}, _
    {ID := 4, IDRole := 3, LastName := "Cops", FirstName := "Gary"} _
}

Dim p As IEnumerable(Of Person) = Sequence.Repeat(Of Person)(people(0), 10)
ObjectDumper.Write(p)
```

Figure 1-25 shows the output for the Listing 1-41.

```
C:\WINDOWS\system32\cmd.exe                                    _ □ ×
ID=1      IDRole=1      LastName=Anderson      FirstName=Brad    ▲
ID=1      IDRole=1      LastName=Anderson      FirstName=Brad
ID=1      IDRole=1      LastName=Anderson      FirstName=Brad
ID=1      IDRole=1      LastName=Anderson      FirstName=Brad
ID=1      IDRole=1      LastName=Anderson      FirstName=Brad
ID=1      IDRole=1      LastName=Anderson      FirstName=Brad
ID=1      IDRole=1      LastName=Anderson      FirstName=Brad
ID=1      IDRole=1      LastName=Anderson      FirstName=Brad
ID=1      IDRole=1      LastName=Anderson      FirstName=Brad
ID=1      IDRole=1      LastName=Anderson      FirstName=Brad
Press any key to continue . . . ▄                               ▼
```

Figure 1-25. The output of Listing 1-41

Quantifier Operators

There are three quantifiers: All, Any, and Contains.

All

This operator uses the predicate function against the elements of a sequence and returns True if all of them satisfy the predicate condition. Let's see the method's prototype:

```
<Extension> _
Public Shared Function All(Of T)(ByVal source As IEnumerable(Of T), _
                         ByVal predicate As Func(Of T, Boolean)) As Boolean
```

The source sequence is enumerated and each element is used against the predicated function condition. If all of them satisfy the predicate condition then a True value is returned. Listing 1-42 uses the predicate to understand if all of sequence's elements are even. The output is Yes, they are.

Listing 1-42. Using the All method to Find Out If All of a Sequence's Elements Are Even

```
Public Class AllExample
    Private Shared Function allFunc(ByVal n As Integer) As Boolean
        Return (n Mod 2 = 0)
    End Function

    Public Sub Listing1_42()
        Dim numbers As Integer() = New Integer() {2, 6, 24, 56, 102}
        Dim allDelegate As New Func(Of Integer, Boolean)(AddressOf allFunc)
```

```
      ObjectDumper.Write(IIf(numbers.All(allDelegate), "Yes, they are", "No, they aren't"))
   End Sub
End Class
```

Any

This operator searches a sequence for elements that satisfy the specified condition.

```
<Extension> _
Public Shared Function Any(Of T)(ByVal source As IEnumerable(Of T)) As Boolean

<Extension> _
Public Shared Function Any(Of T)(ByVal source As IEnumerable(Of T), _
                         ByVal predicate As Func(Of T, Boolean)) As Boolean
```

The predicate function is checked against each element of the source sequence, and stops as soon as the condition is satisfied. When the predicate parameter is not specified, the method returns a True value if the sequence is not empty. Listing 1-43 uses the predicate to understand if at least one element of the numeric sequence is odd. The output is No, there isn't.

Listing 1-43. Using the Any Method to Search for an Odd Numeric Value

```
Public Class AnyExample
   Private Shared Function anyFunc(ByVal n As Integer) As Boolean
      Return (n Mod 2 = 1)
   End Function

   Public Sub Listing1_43()
      Dim numbers As Integer() = New Integer() {2, 6, 24, 56, 102}
      Dim allDelegate As New Func(Of Integer, Boolean)(AddressOf anyFunc)

      ObjectDumper.Write(IIf(numbers.Any(allDelegate), "Yes, they are", "No, they aren't"))
   End Sub
End Class
```

Contains

This operator looks for a specified type within the sequence and returns True when the element is found.

```
<Extension> _
Public Shared Function Contains(Of T)(ByVal source As IEnumerable(Of T), _
```

ByVal value As T) As Boolean

If the source sequence implements the ICollection(Of T) type then its Contains method will be used to search for the specified value. Otherwise the source sequence will be enumerated and each element will be compared to the value parameter until the element is found or the enumeration is over. A True value is returned when the element is found. If no element is found, a False value is returned. Listing 1-44 searches for and finds the number 102 within the sequence, so the output is Yes, there is.

Listing 1-44. The Contains Method Searches for the Specified Value in the Sequence.

```
Dim numbers As Integer() = New Integer() {2, 6, 24, 56, 102}
ObjectDumper.Write(IIf(numbers.Contains(102), "Yes, there is", "No, there isn't"))
```

Equality Operator

There is one equality operator: EqualAll.

EqualAll

This operator compares two sequences and returns True when their elements are equal.

```
<Extension> _
Public Shared Function EqualAll(Of T)(ByVal first As IEnumerable(Of T), _
ByVal second As IEnumerable(Of T)) As Boolean
```

Under the hood the code uses the Equals method provided by the Object type to compare each element of the two sequences side by side. The method will return a True Boolean value if both sequences contain the same elements (see Listing 1-45.)

Listing 1-45. Using the EqualAll Method with Equal and Unequal Sequences

```
Dim sequence1 As Integer() = New Integer() {1, 2, 3, 4, 5}
Dim sequence2 As Integer() = New Integer() {1, 2, 3, 4, 5}
Console.WriteLine("Are those sequences equal?")
ObjectDumper.Write(IIf(sequence1.EqualAll(sequence2), "Yes, they are", "No, they aren't"))
Dim sequence3 As Integer() = New Integer() {5, 2, 3, 4, 1}
Console.WriteLine("Are those sequences equal?")
ObjectDumper.Write(IIf(sequence1.EqualAll(sequence3), "Yes, they are", _
                                        "No, they aren't"))_
```

Listing 1-45 starts comparing two sequences, sequence1 and sequence2. It compares the first element (1) of the first sequence with the first element (1) of the second sequence. Since they are equal, the method moves on to the other elements. The two sequences are equal, so the final output will be Yes, they are.

The next check uses two sequences that are different because the first element of the first sequence (1) is not equal to the first element of the third sequence (5). A False value is returned immediately and the output of the code is No, they aren't.

Set Operators

There are four set operators: Distinct, Intersect, Union, and Except.

Note ➡ The May 2006 CTP version of the LINQ Project doesn't provide support for Nullable elements in the Set operators. This will be implemented in the final version.

Distinct

This operator is similar to the DISTINCT keyword used in SQL; it eliminates duplicates from a sequence.

```
<Extension> _
Public Shared Function Distinct(Of T)(ByVal source As IEnumerable(Of T)) _
                                                As IEnumerable(Of T)
```

When the code processes the query it enumerates the element of the sequence, storing into an IEnumerable(Of T) type each element that has not been stored previously. In Listing 1-46 the Distinct operator selects unique values from the sequence. The output will be 1, 2, 3.

Listing 1-46. The Distinct Operator in Action

```
Dim numbers As Integer() = New Integer() {1, 1, 2, 3, 3}
ObjectDumper.Write(numbers.Distinct())
```

Intersect

This operator returns a sequence made by common elements of two different sequences.

```
<Extension> _
Public Shared Function Intersect(Of T)(ByVal first As IEnumerable(Of T), _
                                ByVal second As IEnumerable(Of T)) _
```

```
                                    As IEnumerable(Of T)
```

The first sequence is enumerated and compared to the second one. Only the common element will be collected and inserted into the IEnumerable(Of T) return type. In Listing 1-47 the Intersect method compares two numeric sequences and returns the common elements: 1 and 3.

Listing 1-47. The Intersect Method Used to Retrieve Common Elements in Two Sequences

```
Dim numbers As Integer() = New Integer() {1, 1, 2, 3, 3}
Dim numbers2 As Integer() = New Integer() {1, 3, 3, 4}
ObjectDumper.Write(numbers.Intersect(numbers2))
```

Union

This operator returns a new sequence formed by uniting the two different sequences.

```
<Extension> _
Public Shared Function Union(Of T)(ByVal first As IEnumerable(Of T), _
                            ByVal second As IEnumerable(Of T)) _
                            As IEnumerable(Of T)
```

The first sequence is enumerated and distinct elements are stored into an IEnumerable(Of T) type. The second sequence is enumerated as well and the elements not stored previously are added to the IEnumerable(Of T) return type. In Listing 1-48 the Union operator returns an IEnumerable(Of Integer) type composed of distinct elements from the two numeric sequences: 1, 3, 2, and 4.

Listing 1-48. The Union Operator in Action

```
Dim numbers As Integer() = New Integer() {1, 1, 2, 3, 3}
Dim numbers2 As Integer() = New Integer() {1, 3, 3, 4}
ObjectDumper.Write(numbers.Union(numbers2))
```

Note ➡ The Union operator doesn't sort the numbers when it produces the IEnumerable(Of T) return type.

Except

This operator produces a new sequence composed of the elements of the first sequence not present in the second sequence.

```
<Extension> _
Public Shared Function Except(Of T)(ByVal first As IEnumerable(Of T), _
                          ByVal second As IEnumerable(Of T)) _
                                   As IEnumerable(Of T)
```

When the code processes the query expression it starts to enumerate the first sequence, storing its distinct elements in an IEnumerable(Of T) type. Then it enumerates the second sequence and removes the common elements into the IEnumerable(Of T) type stored previously. Finally, it returns the processed IEnumerable(Of T) type to the caller. The output for the example shown in Listing 1-49 is 2, 4.

Listing 1-49. The Except Method in Action

```
Dim numbers As Integer() = New Integer() {1, 2, 3, 4}
Dim numbers2 As Integer() = New Integer() {1, 1, 3, 3}
ObjectDumper.Write(numbers.Except(numbers2))
```

Conversion Operators

There are seven conversion operators: OfType, Cast, ToSequence, ToArray, ToList, ToDictionary, and ToLookup.

OfType

This operator produces a new IEnumerable(Of T) type composed of only the element of the specified type.

```
<Extension> _
Public Shared Function OfType(Of T)(ByVal source As IEnumerable) As IEnumerable(Of T)
```

The operator enumerates the elements of the source sequence, searching for those whose type is equal to T. Only those elements will be inserted in the final IEnumerable(Of T) sequence that the OfType method returns. Listing 1-50 searches for the elements of Double type in the sequence. The result is 2.0.

Listing 1-50. The OfType Searches for the Specified Type T in the Sequence.

```
Dim sequence As Object() = New Object() {1, "Hello", 2.0}
ObjectDumper.Write(sequence.OfType(Of Double)())
```

Cast

This operator casts the elements of the sequence to a given type.

```
<Extension> _
Public Shared Function Cast(Of T)(ByVal source As IEnumerable) As IEnumerable(Of T)
```

The operator enumerates the elements of the source sequence and casts its elements to the T type. Those new elements are collected into a new IEnumerable(Of T) type that will be returned. Listing 1-51 casts Object type to Double type. The output will be 1.0, 2.0, 3.0.

Listing 1-51. The Cast Operator in Action

```
Dim doubles As Object() = New Object() {1.0, 2.0, 3.0}
ObjectDumper.Write(doubles.Cast(Of Double)())
```

ToSequence

This operator simply returns the typed sequence to a given IEnumerable(Of T) type.

```
<Extension> _
Public Shared Function ToSequence(Of T)(ByVal source As IEnumerable(Of T)) _
                                            As IEnumerable(Of T)
```

This operator has no effect on the source sequence other than changing the type to IEnumerable(Of T). This could be useful to call a standard query expression when a type implements its own query-expression methods.

ToArray

This operator returns an array composed of the elements of the source sequence.

```
<Extension> _
Public Shared Function ToArray(Of T)(ByVal source As IEnumerable(Of T)) As T()
```

In Listing 1-52 the elements of the people sequence that have the LastName length equal to 4 are retrieved and inserted into a String array.

Listing 1-52 does not use the ObjectDumper's Write method; eliminating it allowed me to demonstrate more clearly that the result of the query has been converted into an array. The output is Gray, Cops.

Listing 1-52. The Query Result Is Inserted into an Array Using the ToArray Operator.

```
Dim people As List(Of Person) = New List(Of Person) { _
    {ID := 1, IDRole := 1, LastName := "Anderson", FirstName := "Brad"}, _
    {ID := 2, IDRole := 2, LastName := "Gray", FirstName := "Tom"}, _
    {ID := 3, IDRole := 2, LastName := "Grant", FirstName := "Mary"}, _
    {ID := 4, IDRole := 3, LastName := "Cops", FirstName := "Gary"} _
}

Dim query = From p In people _
    Where p.LastName.Length = 4 _
    Select p.LastName

Dim names As String() = query.ToArray()

For Dim i As Integer = 0 To names.Length - 1
    Console.WriteLine(names(i))
Next
```

ToList

This operator returns a List(Of T) type composed of the elements of the source sequence.

```
<Extension> _
Public Shared Function ToList(Of T)(ByVal source As IEnumerable(Of T)) As List(Of T)
```

In Listing 1-53 the result of the query is converted into a List(Of String) type. The output of this code snippet is Gray, Cops.

Listing 1-53. The ToList Method in Action

```
Dim query = From p In people _
    Where p.LastName.Length = 4 _
    Select p.LastName

Dim names As List(Of String) = query.ToList(Of String)()
ObjectDumper.Write(names)
```

ToDictionary

This operator returns a Dictionary(Of K, E) type composed of the elements of a sequence.

```
<Extension> _
Public Shared Function ToDictionary(Of T, K)(ByVal source As IEnumerable(Of T), _
                                    ByVal keySelector As Func(Of T, K)) _
                                            As Dictionary(Of K, T)


<Extension> _
Public Shared Function ToDictionary(Of T, K)(ByVal source As IEnumerable(Of T), _
                                    ByVal keySelector As Func(Of T, K), _
                                    ByVal comparer As IEqualityComparer(Of K)) _
                                    As Dictionary(Of K, T)


<Extension> _
Public Shared Function ToDictionary(Of T, K, E)(ByVal source As IEnumerable(Of T), _
ByVal keySelector As Func(Of T, K), ByVal elementSelector As Func(Of T, E)) _
As Dictionary(Of K, E)


<Extension> _
Public Shared Function ToDictionary(Of T, K, E)(ByVal source As IEnumerable(Of T), _
                                    ByVal keySelector As Func(Of T, K), _
                                    ByVal elementSelector As Func(Of T, E), _
                                    ByVal comparer As IEqualityComparer(Of K))

                                            As Dictionary(Of K, E)
```

The prototype with both keySelector and elementSelector parameters is used to specify the elements of the sequence promoted to be the dictionary's key and value, respectively. When the elementSelector parameter is omitted the value will be the element itself. Finally, the prototype with the comparer parameter allows us to define a custom comparer function used during the Dictionary(Of K, E) type construction.

In Listing 1-54 .NET Reflection and LINQ are used to retrieve the Integer type's methods, which will be inserted into a Dictionary(Of String, Integer) type.

Listing 1-54. Using ToDictionary() to Retrieve a Dictionary(Of String, integer) Type

```
Public Class ToDictionaryExample
    Private Shared Function getKey(ByVal k As IGrouping(Of String, MethodInfo)) As String
        Return k.Key
    End Function

    Private Shared Function getCount(ByVal k As IGrouping(Of String, MethodInfo)) As Integer
        Return k.Count()
    End Function
```

```
Public Sub Listing1_54()
    Dim keyDelegate As New Func(Of IGrouping(Of String, MethodInfo), String) _
                            (AddressOf getKey)
    Dim countDelegate As New Func(Of IGrouping(Of String, MethodInfo), Integer) _
                            (AddressOf getCount)

    Dim q = From m In GetType(Integer).GetMethods() _
        Group By m.Name _
        Select it

    Dim d As Dictionary(Of String, Integer) = _
                                Sequence.ToDictionary(Of _
                                IGrouping(Of String, MethodInfo), String, Integer)

    _
                                (q, keyDelegate, countDelegate)


End Sub
End Class
```

The query groups the methods of the Integer type. The ToDictionary() method is used to retrieve a dictionary with keys equal to the methods' name, and values equal to the methods' overloads number.

ToLookup

This operator returns a Lookup(Of K, T) type composed of elements from the source sequence.

```
<Extension> _
Public Shared Function ToList(Of T)(ByVal source As IEnumerable(Of T)) As List(Of T)

<Extension> _
Public Shared Function ToLookup(Of T, K)(ByVal source As IEnumerable(Of T), _
                                ByVal keySelector As Func(Of T, K)) _
                                                As Lookup(Of K, T)

<Extension> _
Public Shared Function ToLookup(Of T, K)(ByVal source As IEnumerable(Of T), _
                                ByVal keySelector As Func(Of T, K), _
                                ByVal comparer As IEqualityComparer(Of K)) _
                                                As Lookup(Of K, T)
```

```
<Extension> _
Public Shared Function ToLookup(Of T, K, E)(ByVal source As IEnumerable(Of T), _
                                    ByVal keySelector As Func(Of T, K), _
                                    ByVal elementSelector As Func(Of T, E)) _
                                                As Lookup(Of K, E)


<Extension> _
Public Shared Function ToLookup(Of T, K, E)(ByVal source As IEnumerable(Of T), _
                                    ByVal keySelector As Func(Of T, K), _
                                    ByVal elementSelector As Func(Of T, E), _
                                    ByVal comparer As IEqualityComparer(Of K)) _
                                                As Lookup(Of K, E)
```

This new Lookup(Of K, T) type differs from the Dictionary(Of K, E) type in the implementation of the type itself. The former allows us to associate a key with a sequence of values. The latter allows us to associate a key with a single value.

The prototype with both keySelector and elementSelector parameters is used to specify the elements of the sequence promoted to be the lookup's key and value, respectively. When the elementSelector parameter is omitted the value will be the element itself. Finally, the prototype with the comparer parameter allows us to define a custom comparer function used during the Lookup(Of K, T) type construction.

Listing 1-55 creates a Lookup(Of string, Salary) type whose key is equal to the Year element of the salaries sequence; the related value is the salary element itself.

Listing 1-55. The ToLookup Method Converts the Query Expression Result into a Lookup(Of String, Salary) Type.

```
Dim people As List(Of Person) = New List(Of Person) { _
    {ID := 1, IDRole := 1, LastName := "Anderson", FirstName := "Brad"}, _
    {ID := 2, IDRole := 2, LastName := "Gray", FirstName := "Tom"}, _
    {ID := 3, IDRole := 2, LastName := "Grant", FirstName := "Mary"}, _
    {ID := 4, IDRole := 3, LastName := "Cops", FirstName := "Gary"} _
}

Dim salaries As New List(Of Salary) { _
    {IDPerson := 1, Year := 2004, SalaryYear := 10000.0}, _
    {IDPerson := 1, Year := 2005, SalaryYear := 15000.0}, _
    {IDPerson := 2, Year := 2005, SalaryYear := 15000.0} _
}

Public Class ToLookupExample
    Private Shared Function yearKey(ByVal k As Salary) As String
        Return k.Year.ToString
```

```
    End Function

    Private Shared Function getSalary(ByVal k As Salary) As Salary
        Return k
    End Function


    Public Sub Listing1_55(ByVal people As List(Of Person), ByVal salaries As List(Of Salary))
        Dim yearDelegate As New Func(Of Salary, String)(AddressOf yearKey)
        Dim salaryDelegate As New Func(Of Salary, Salary)(AddressOf getSalary)

        Dim q As IEnumerable(Of Salary) = From p In people, s In salaries _
            Where p.ID = 1 AndAlso p.ID = s.IDPerson _
            Select s

        Dim d As Lookup(Of String, Salary) = _
                    Sequence.ToLookup(Of Salary, String, Salary)(q, yearDelegate, salaryDelegate)
    End Sub
End Class
```

Summary

This long chapter covered the two main parts of LINQ to Objects.

First you examined the new VB 9.0 features to support LINQ. You saw how extension methods extend existing .NET types with new methods. You also saw other new features, such as anonymous types and object initialization expressions.

Then you examined all the standard query operators and saw them in code examples to understand their functionality.

The next chapter covers LINQ to SQL, which is dedicated to querying information from relational databases such as Microsoft SQL Server. The query expression syntax you learned in this chapter is also used to query databases.

CHAPTER 2

LINQ to ADO.NET

This chapter covers the following:

Mapping LINQ to databases. Classes, properties, and attributes tell LINQ about database tables.

The DataContext class. This class supports LINQ's ORM functionality.

Advanced features. LINQ to SQL supports advanced database features such as transactions, optimist concurrency, stored procedure calls, and more.

LINQ to SQL in Visual Studio. Support for LINQ to SQL, including IntelliSense and debugging, are added to Visual Studio when LINQ is installed.

LINQ to DataSet. LINQ to SQL is integrated into ADO.NET, specifically with DataSet objects.

Introduction

In Chapter 1 we focused on the standard query operators, looking closely at each method for querying and modifying objects. You now know everything needed to query any data source. Whether data sources are in-memory objects, relational databases, or XML, we use the same uniform syntax to query them. An object is queryable as long as it implements the IQueryable(Of T) or IEnumerable(Of T) interface.

LINQ to SQL implements the IQueryable(Of T) interface to convert query expressions into Expression trees, which it transforms into SQL statements.

Results are stored using a basic ORM model, so rows are placed in objects created in our code. The LINQ to SQL run-time infrastructure can track each change to our objects. To persist changes, we call a method, and every tracked change will be propagated to the database.

LINQ to SQL is compatible with ADO.NET 2.0 classes such as Connection and DataSet. You can easily integrate LINQ to SQL with existing ADO.NET programs; hence this chapter's title.

Database Interaction

LINQ to SQL introduces LINQ functionality for Microsoft SQL Server 2000 and 2005. Thanks to the IQueryable(Of T) interface, it's theoretically possible to create providers for other databases; at this stage it's not easy, but in the final release a more complete provider framework is expected.

LINQ to SQL defines new C# attributes, properties, and classes to let us interact with SQL Server databases by mapping database objects to objects in our programs. Three basic steps are required:

1. Create classes for the tables in the database that you want to use, decorating them with appropriate LINQ attributes.

2. Decorate the fields and properties in these classes so LINQ can use them and knows how to use them.

3. Create a DataContext object to mediate between the database tables and the classes that map to them.

The next three sections provide examples of each step.

Mapping a Class to a Database Table

Mapping a class to a database table allows us to use LINQ against the table. The Table attribute, defined in the System.Data.DLinq namespace, informs LINQ about how to map a class to a database table.

Note ➤ In this chapter we use a database called People, which has the same structure as the data source in Chapter 1. This allows you to focus on LINQ features and not on database complexities. Instructions for creating the database are included in the downloadable source code from the Source Code/Download area of www.apress.com. To run the code examples, you must create the People database first.

The following code simply declares a new public class named Person and associates it with the Person database table.

```
<Table(Name:="Person")> _
Partial Public Class Person
```

The Table attribute's Name property is optional. LINQ uses the class name as the default table name.

Mapping Fields and Properties to Table Columns

Mapping fields and properties to table columns makes the columns available to LINQ. Figure 2-1 shows the Person table's structure. We want to make all the columns available to LINQ as properties of the Person class. Note that the first column is the primary key. It's also an IDENTITY column, so SQL Server automatically sets its value.

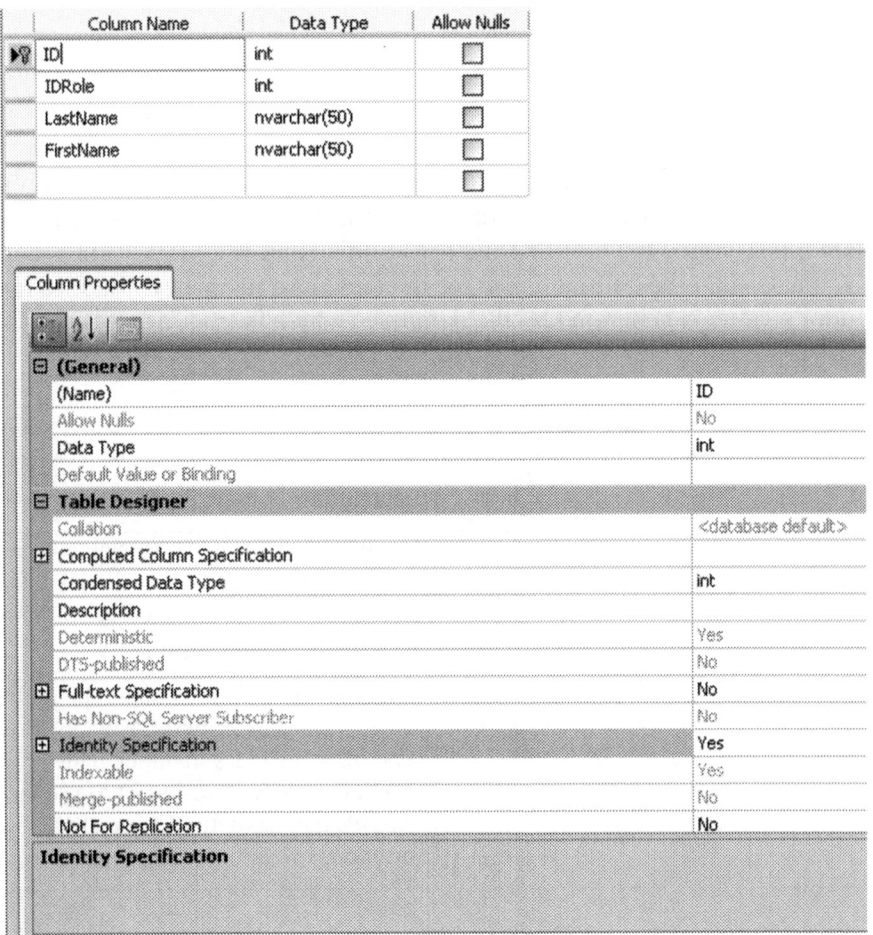

Figure 2-1. The Person table's structure

For each column we want to use with LINQ, we need to declare a property and decorate it with the Column attribute. Since we're using properties, we also declare private fields for the underlying data. For the first column, ID, we declare a field, _ID, and a property, ID.

```
<Table(Name:="Person")> _
Partial Public Class Person
     Private _ID As Integer

  <Column(DBType:="Int NOT NULL IDENTITY", Id:=true, AutoGen:=true)> _
  Public Property ID() As Integer
    Get
      Return Me._ID
    End Get
    Set
       Me._ID = value
    End Set
  End Property
```

The Column attribute has eight properties (see Table 2-1), all of which are optional. We've used five of them. Name specifies the column name. DBType specifies not only the column's data type (Integer) but also that it's not nullable and is an IDENTITY column. The Id property indicates that the column is part of the table's primary key. AutoGen indicates that the column's value is generated by the database (which is true for all IDENTITY columns).

Table 2-1. Column-Attribute Properties

Property	Description
AutoGen	Identifies a column whose value is generated by the database. Usually we will use this property in conjunction with primary key columns defined with the IDENTITY property.
DBType	Specifies the column's data type in the database. If you omit this property, LINQ will infer the type from the class member. This property is mandatory only if you want to use the CreateDatabase method to create a new database instance.

Property	Description
Id	Specifies that a column is part of a table's primary (or unique) key. LINQ currently works only with tables that have primary (or unique) keys.
IsDiscriminator	Indicates that the member holds the discriminator value for an inheritance hierarchy.
IsVersion	Indicates the member is a database timestamp or version number.
Name	Specifies the column's name in the database. Defaults to the member name.
Storage	Specifies the name of the private field underlying a property. LINQ will bypass the property's get and set accessors and use the field instead.
UpdateCheck	Specifies how LINQ detects optimistic concurrency conflicts. The possible values are Always, Never, and WhenChanged. If no member is marked with IsVersion=True, all members participate in detection unless explicitly specified otherwise.

By default, LINQ uses a property's Set and Get accessors, but we can override this with the Storage property. For example, if we add the Storage property to the Column attribute for ID as follows, LINQ will use the underlying private field, _ID, instead of the accessors.

```
<Table(Name:="Person")> _
Partial Public Class Person
     Private _ID As Integer

 <Column(Storage:="_ID", DBType:="Int NOT NULL IDENTITY", Id:=true, AutoGen:=true)> _
 Public Property ID() As Integer
   Get
     Return Me._ID
   End Get
   Set
      Me._ID = value
   End Set
 End Property
```

Now declare the private fields and public properties for the rest of the columns. The full class code is in Listing 2-1.

Listing 2-1. The Person Class Mapped to the Person Table in the People Database

```
<Table(Name:="Person")> _
Partial Public Class Person

  Private _ID As Integer

  Private _IDRole As Integer

  Private _LastName As String

  Private _FirstName As String

  Private _Role As EntityRef(Of Role)

  Public Sub New()
   MyBase.New
   Me._Role = CType(Nothing, EntityRef(Of Role))
  End Sub

  <Column(Storage:="_ID", DBType:="Int NOT NULL IDENTITY", Id:=true, AutoGen:=true)> _
  Public Property ID() As Integer
   Get
     Return Me._ID
   End Get
   Set
      Me._ID = value
   End Set
  End Property

  <Column(Storage:="_IDRole", DBType:="Int NOT NULL")> _
  Public Property IDRole() As Integer
   Get
     Return Me._IDRole
   End Get
   Set
      Me._IDRole = value
   End Set
  End Property

  <Column(Storage:="_LastName", DBType:="NVarChar(50) NOT NULL")> _
  Public Property LastName() As String
```

```
    Get
      Return Me._LastName
    End Get
    Set
       Me._LastName = value
    End Set
  End Property

  <Column(Storage:="_FirstName", DBType:="NVarChar(50) NOT NULL")> _
  Public Property FirstName() As String
    Get
      Return Me._FirstName
    End Get
    Set
       Me._FirstName = value
    End Set
  End Property
End Class
```

Creating a Data Context

A *data context* is an object of type System.Data.Dlinq.DataContext. It supports database retrieval and update for objects known to LINQ. It handles the database connection and implements the SQO for database access. To use tables in LINQ, they must not only be mapped but must also be available in a data context. You can make them available in two ways.

One way is to create a data context and then use it to create an object that LINQ can use as a table. For example, the two lines

```
Dim PeopleDataContext As New DataContext(connString)
Dim People As Table(Of Person) = PeopleDataContext.GetTable(Of Person)()
```

create a data context, PeopleDataContext, and a Table collection, People (for the Person database table), available in that context.

A new generic collection class, Table(Of T), in the System.Data.DLinq namespace, is used to represent database tables. We used the data context's GetTable(Of T) method to create a People object of type Table(Of Person) in the PeopleDataContext context. The argument to the DataContext constructor is the same thing you provide an ADO.NET connection. Here is an example:

```
Dim connString As String = "Data Source=.;Initial Catalog=People;" & _
"Integrated Security=True"
```

The result is that our database is known to LINQ as PeopleDataContext and the Person table is known as People.

Note ► The Table(Of T) generic collection type implements IEnumerable(Of T) and IQueryable(Of T) as well as ITable, which implements both IEnumerable and IQueryable.

The other—and recommended—way is to use a *strongly typed data context*, like the following:

```
Partial Public Class People
  Inherits DataContext

  Public Persons As Table(Of Person)
  Public Sub New(ByVal connection As String)
    MyBase.New(connection)
  End Sub
End Class
```

In this example we declare a class, PeopleDataContext, to represent the data context. The class has a field, People, for the database table Person. The constructor calls the DataContext base constructor with the connection string.

To use the strongly typed context, we'd instantiate it before performing our first query, like this:

```
Dim people As New PeopleDataContext(connString)
```

In this case our database is known to LINQ as people and the Person table is known as People.

We've now written all we need for LINQ to manage the Person database table as the People collection. Querying it will be similar to what we did in Chapter 1 to query in-memory objects.

Querying a Database with LINQ to SQL

The only difference in querying a database with respect to an in-memory object is that we need to instantiate our data context before our first query. In Listing 2-2, the first line of code in Main() does this.

Listing 2-2. The Main Class Containing the Code to Query the Database

```
Dim people = New PeopleDataContext()
Dim tablePeople = people.People
Dim tableSalaries = people.Salaries

Dim query = From p In tablePeople, s In tableSalaries _
```

```
    Where p.ID = s.ID _
    Select New {p.LastName, p.FirstName, s.Year, s.SalaryYear}

For Each Dim record In query
    Console.WriteLine("Name: {0}, {1} - Year: {2}", record.LastName, _
                                          record.FirstName, _
                                          record.Year)

    Console.WriteLine("Salary: {0}", record.SalaryYear)
Next
```

The DataContext is the two-way channel by which LINQ queries the database and the results are turned into objects. Figure 2-2 shows the output of the code in Listing 2-2.

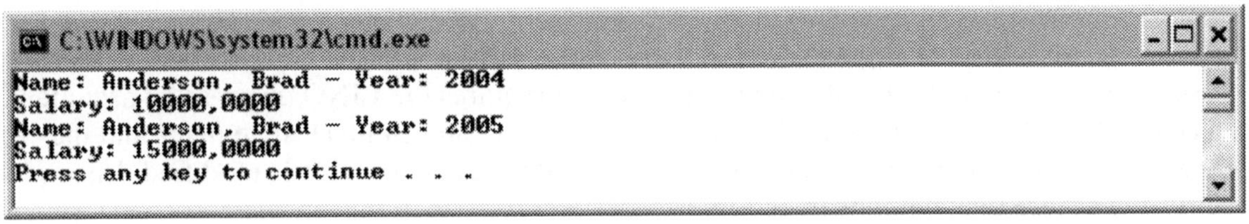

Figure 2-2. The output is similar to examples from Chapter1, but this time data is retrieved from a SQL Server database.

The DataContext class transforms the LINQ query into a SQL query. The Log property of the DataContext class is an easy way to determine the SQL query sent to the database. See the code snippet in Listing 2-3:

Listing 2-3. Displaying the SQL Query Sent by the Data Context

```
Dim people = New PeopleDataContext()
Dim tablePeople = people.People
Dim tableSalaries = people.Salaries

people.Log = Console.Out

Dim query = From p In tablePeople, s In tableSalaries _
    Where p.ID = s.ID _
    Select New {p.LastName, p.FirstName, s.Year, s.SalaryYear}

For Each Dim record In query
    Console.WriteLine("Name: {0}, {1} - Year: {2}", record.LastName, _
                                          record.FirstName, _
                                          record.Year)

    Console.WriteLine("Salary: {0}", record.SalaryYear)
Next
```

The second line redirects the log to the console, as shown in Figure 2-3.

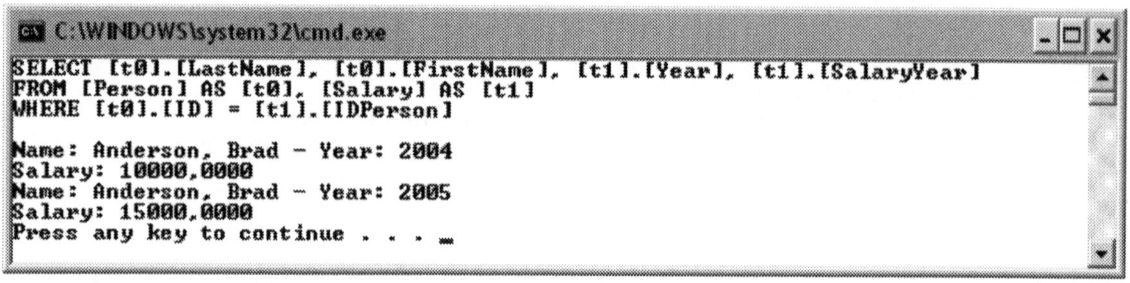

Figure 2-3. A SQL query sent by a data context

There are two other ways to see the SQL sent by LINQ. Use the GetQueryText method of DataContext to see SELECT statements. The method requires the LINQ query as an argument. The GetChangeText method is used for INSERT, UPDATE, and DELETE statements and the SQL is generated only after an object associated with a database table is modified. Listing 2-4 shows these two methods in action.

Listing 2-4. Using GetQueryText and GetChangeText Methods to View SQL Statements

```
Dim people = New PeopleDataContext()
Dim tablePeople = people.People
Dim tableSalaries = people.Salaries

Dim query = From p In tablePeople, s In tableSalaries _
    Where p.ID = s.ID _
    Select New {p.LastName, p.FirstName, s.Year, s.SalaryYear}

Console.WriteLine(people.GetQueryText(query))
Console.WriteLine()

For Each Dim record In query
    Console.WriteLine("Name: {0}, {1} - Year: {2}", record.LastName, _
                                                record.FirstName, _
                                                record.Year)
    Console.WriteLine("Salary: {0}", record.SalaryYear)
Next

Dim person As New Person()
Person.IDRole = 1
Person.FirstName = "From"
Person.LastName = "Code"

people.People.Add(Person)

Console.WriteLine()
Console.WriteLine(people.GetChangeText())
```

As you can see from the output shown in Figure 2-4, the INSERT statement is followed by a SELECT instruction useful for retrieving the new row identifier contained in the @@IDENTITY T-SQL variable.

```
C:\WINDOWS\system32\cmd.exe                                        - □ ×
SELECT [t0].[LastName], [t0].[FirstName], [t1].[Year], [t1].[SalaryYear]
FROM [Person] AS [t0], [Salary] AS [t1]
WHERE [t0].[ID] = [t1].[IDPerson]

Name: Anderson, Brad - Year: 2004
Salary: 10000.0000
Name: Anderson, Brad - Year: 2005
Salary: 15000.0000

INSERT INTO [Person](FirstName, LastName, IDRole) VALUES(@p0, @p1, @p2)
SELECT [t0].[ID]
FROM [Person] AS [t0]
WHERE [t0].[ID] = (CONVERT(Int,@@IDENTITY))

Press any key to continue . . .
```

Figure 2-4. Two other ways to retrieve the SQL statements built by LINQ

The INSERT statement is built by LINQ because the code adds a new row into the People entity class contained in the PeopleDataContext class.

Adding, Modifying, and Deleting Rows

As you can see in Listing 2-4, adding a new row consists of creating an object of a class that maps to a table, setting its values, and calling the Add method on the appropriate Table(Of T) instance.

This is a classic object-oriented approach—adding an object to a collection—but this time you're adding a row to a database table! You don't write any SQL; everything is handled transparently by the data context. However, nothing happens in the database until you call the SubmitChanges method shown in Listing 2-5.

Listing 2-5. The SubmitChanges Method Propagates Changes to the Database.

```
Dim people = New PeopleDataContext()

Dim person As New Person()
Person.IDRole = 1
Person.FirstName = "From"
Person.LastName = "Code"
people.People.Add(Person)

people.SubmitChanges()
```

```
Dim query = From p In people.People _
    Select p

For Each Dim record In query
    Console.WriteLine("Name: {0}, {1}", record.LastName, record.FirstName)
Next
```

After the Add method has modified the Person table with a new row, the SubmitChanges() method will contact the database and will execute the related SQL statement. Also, the method will be able to substitute the generic @p0, @p1, and @p2 placeholders with the related value contained in the object. The output in Figure 2-5 shows that a new row has been added into the database.

Figure 2-5. A new row has been added from the code.

Now you'll learn to modify and delete rows. To modify a row, we first have to retrieve the row and change the values, as in Listing 2-6.

Listing 2-6. Modifing a Row with LINQ to SQL

```
Public Class UpdateExample
    Public Shared Function whereCondition(ByVal p As Person) As Boolean
        Return p.ID = 5
    End Function

    Sub Listing2_6()
        Dim people = New PeopleDataContext()
        Dim predicateDelegate As New Func(Of Person, Boolean)(AddressOf whereCondition)

        Dim person = people.People.Single(predicateDelegate)

        person.FirstName = "Name"
        person.LastName = "Modified"

        Console.WriteLine(people.GetChangeText())

        people.SubmitChanges()

    End Sub
```

End Class

In the code snippet, using the Single method we retrieve the unique row whose ID is equal to 5. Then we change some attributes and call SubmitChanges() to update the database table. Figure 2-6 shows the SQL generated by LINQ.

```
C:\WINDOWS\system32\cmd.exe                                                    _ □ ×
UPDATE [Person]
SET [FirstName] = @p4, [LastName] = @p5
FROM [Person]
WHERE ([FirstName] = @p0) AND ([LastName] = @p1) AND ([IDRole] = @p2) AND ([ID]
= @p3)
SELECT NULL AS [EMPTY]
FROM [Person] AS [t1]
WHERE ((@@ROWCOUNT) > 0) AND ([t1].[ID] = @p6)

Press any key to continue . . . _
```

Figure 2-6. The UPDATE statement built by LINQ to SQL

As you can see, LINQ produces an UPDATE statement containing only the columns changed in the code. The last SELECT is useful for retrieving the number of rows affected by the updating process.

Deleting a row is an easier process that doesn't involve a round trip to the database to first retrieve the row. We can use the Remove method of the DataContext class, and specify the object previously set with the identifier value that we want to remove from the table. Listing 2-7 shows the code.

Listing 2-7. Using the Remove Method to Delete a Row from the Database

```
Dim people = New PeopleDataContext()

Dim person As New Person()
person.ID = 5

people.People.Remove(person)

Console.WriteLine(people.GetChangeText())

people.SubmitChanges()
```

The code creates a new Person object and sets its primary key to the value of the row we are going to remove. Finally, the object is passed to the Remove method and the changes are submitted with the SubmitChanges() method call.

DataContext: Advanced Features

We've focused our attention on the basic features provided by LINQ to SQL (in the System.Data.DLinq.dll assembly). Data contexts have even more features. In the next sections you'll see how to define relationships between entities, and the benefits of doing that.

Defining Relationships Between Entities

The first feature we'll look at regards relationships between tables. A relational database such as Microsoft SQL Server provides the capability to define a relationship between two tables using primary and foreign keys. For example, a table containing a list of orders could have a foreign key pointing to a customers table. Using this relationship we can easily retrieve all the records for a specific customer. Moreover, we can define the rules to apply to the rows of related tables when some action occurs. For example, we can inform the database to remove every order row for a customer when the related customer is removed.

The relationships between objects are defined in a different way. Usually a class contains a collection of related objects from another class.

LINQ to SQL provides a relational-like way to define a relationship between two entity classes. Thanks to new generic types such as EntitySet(Of T) and EntityRef(Of T), it's possible to define the class members that are involved in relationships.

The steps to implement relationships between entity classes are as follows:

1. Add an EntitySet(Of T) private field in the parent entity class to collect the objects belonging to the child entity class.

2. Add the property that encapsulates the access to this private field. Additionally, we have to add the Association decoration to specify some properties, such as the relation name and the keys involved in the relation.

3. Add the initialization of this private field using its two-parameter constructor.

4. Add an EntityRef(Of T) private field in the child entity class to retrieve the instance of the parent entity object.

5. Add the property that encapsulates the access to this private field. Again, we have to add the Association attribute to the property.

6. Add the initialization of this private field using the default constructor.

In the People database, the Person table has a foreign key, IDRole, pointing to the primary key of the Role table. Using the LINQ to SQL Association attribute (in the System.Data.DLinq namespace) with the Role and Person class definitions, we can specify this kind of relationship between these tables in our code. Let's apply these steps to the Role and Person classes. Listing 2-8 gives the code for the parent entity class, Role.

Listing 2-8. The Role Entity Class

```
<Table(Name:="Role")> _
Public Class Role

    ' Fields
    Private _Description As String
    Private _ID As Integer
    Private _People As EntitySet(Of Person)

    ' Methods
    Public Sub New()
        Me._People = New EntitySet(Of Person) _
                    (New Notification(Of Person) _
                    (AddressOf Me.Attach_Person), _
                    New Notification(Of Person) _
                    (AddressOf Me.Detach_Person))
    End Sub

    <Association(Name:="FK_Person_Role", Storage:="_People", OtherKey:="IDRole")> _
    Public Property People() As EntitySet(Of Person)
        Get
            Return Me._People
        End Get
        Set(ByVal value As EntitySet(Of Person))
            Me._People.Assign(value)
        End Set
    End Property

    Private Sub Attach_Person(ByVal entity As Person)
        entity.Role = Me
    End Sub

    Private Sub Detach_Person(ByVal entity As Person)
        entity.Role = Nothing
    End Sub
    <Column(Name:="ID", Storage:="_ID", _
            DbType:="int NOT NULL IDENTITY", _
            ID:=True, AutoGen:=True)> _
    Public Property ID() As Integer
        Get
            Return Me._ID
        End Get
        Set(ByVal value As Integer)
```

```
        Me._ID = value
      End Set
   End Property

   <Column(Name:="RoleDescription", Storage:="_Description", _
         DbType:="nvarchar NOT NULL")>_
   Public Property RoleDescription() As String
      Get
         Return Me._Description
      End Get
      Set(ByVal value As String)
         Me._Description = value
      End Set
   End Property
End Class
```

The Role entity class represents the parent table. That's why it has

```
Private _People As EntitySet(Of Person)
```

which contains the People objects that belong to a role.

The Role class has to define a public property that encapsulates the access code to the EntitySet(Of Person) private field. Here is the code snippet for it:

```
   <Association(Name:="FK_Person_Role", Storage:="_People", OtherKey:="IDRole")> _
   Public Property People() As EntitySet(Of Person)
      Get
         Return Me._People
      End Get
      Set(ByVal value As EntitySet(Of Person))
         Me._People.Assign(value)
      End Set
   End Property
```

The Assign method of EntitySet(Of T) sets the new value in the collection so that the new object is monitored by LINQ to SQL and by its change-tracking service.

The Association attribute informs LINQ to SQL about the relationship name, the private field used to store the Person objects collection, and the foreign key in the related table. The Association attribute provides the ThisKey property too (see Table 2-2 for the full list of properties). It represents the parent-table key related to the OtherKey. In our example, ThisKey has been omitted because it coincides with the primary key and LINQ to SQL is able to infer its name automatically.

Table 2-2. The Full List of the Association Attribute's Properties

Property	Description
Name	Identifies the name of the relation. Usually its value is the same as the name of the foreign key constraint relation name defined in the database. You have to specify it if you plan to use the CreateDatabase() method from the DataContext class to create a new database with this relation. You have to use the same name in the entity class that composes the relation with this one.
IsParent	When set to True this property indicates that the related entity class is the parent class.
OtherKey	Identifies a list of parent entity class keys separated by commas. If the keys are not specified, LINQ to SQL infers them and assumes they are equal to the primary keys defined in the parent entity class.
Storage	Storage contains the name of the private field defined in the class. When specifying this property, LINQ to SQL will use the class's field to access data instead of using the related Get and Set accessors.
ThisKey	Identifies a list of keys of this entity class, separated by commas. If the keys are not specified, LINQ to SQL assumes they are equal to the primary keys defined in this class.
Unique	When set to True this property indicates that there will be a one-to-one relationship between entities.

The next step is to initialize the private field using the Role class constructor:

```
Public Sub New()
    Me._People = New EntitySet(Of Person) _
            (New Notification(Of Person) _
            (AddressOf Me.Attach_Person), _
            New Notification(Of Person) _
            (AddressOf Me.Detach_Person))
```

End Sub

We pass two delegate methods to the EntitySet(Of T) constructor. The Attach_Person method will set the related Role object to the new Person object. The Detach_Person method will set to Nothing the related Role object in the Person object:

```
Private Sub Attach_Person(ByVal entity As Person)
   entity.Role = Me
End Sub

Private Sub Detach_Person(ByVal entity As Person)
   entity.Role = Nothing
End Sub
```

In the child entity class related to the Person database table, we add a private EntityRef(Of Role) field so we'll be able to retrieve its role simply:

Console.WriteLine(**person.Role.RoleDescription**)

Next we have to add a public property containing the accessors to get and set the private field value. In accordance with the steps listed earlier, we have to use the Association attribute even with this public property. Here we should define the same name used in the earlier example because LINQ to SQL has to know that we are going to define the other side of the relation. Moreover, using the ThisKey property we can specify the column name of the child entity class related to the foreign key column of the database table. Finally, the IsParent property set to True indicates that the related entity class is the parent class.

Listing 2-9 shows how to modify the Person class to define the relationship with the Role class:

Listing 2-9. The Person Class Modified to Include the Relationship with the Role Class

```
<Table(Name:="Person")> _
Public Class Person
   ' Methods
   Public Sub New()
      Me._Role = New EntityRef(Of Role)
   End Sub


   ' Properties
   <Column(Name:="FirstName", Storage:="_firstName", DbType:="nvarchar NOT NULL")> _
   Public Property FirstName() As String
      Get
         Return Me._firstName
      End Get
      Set(ByVal value As String)
         Me._firstName = value
      End Set
```

```vb
End Property

<Column(Name:="ID", Storage:="_ID", _
         DbType:="int NOT NULL IDENTITY", _
         Id:=True, AutoGen:=True)> _
Public Property ID() As Integer
   Get
      Return Me._ID
   End Get
   Set(ByVal value As Integer)
      Me._ID = value
   End Set
End Property

<Column(Name:="IDRole", Storage:="_IDRole", DbType:="int NOT NULL")> _
Public Property IDRole() As Integer
   Get
      Return Me._IDRole
   End Get
   Set(ByVal value As Integer)
      Me._IDRole = value
   End Set
End Property

<Column(Name:="LastName", Storage:="_lastName", DbType:="nvarchar NOT NULL")> _
Public Property LastName() As String
   Get
      Return Me._lastName
   End Get
   Set(ByVal value As String)
      Me._lastName = value
   End Set
End Property

<Association(Name:="FK_Person_Role", Storage:="_Role", _
             ThisKey:="IDRole", IsParent:=True)> _
Public Property Role() As Role
   Get
      Return Me._Role.Entity
   End Get
   Set(ByVal value As Role)
      Dim role1 As Role = Me._Role.Entity
      If (Not role1 Is value) Then
         If (Not role1 Is Nothing) Then
            Me._Role.Entity = Nothing
            role1.People.Remove(Me)
         End If
         Me._Role.Entity = value
         If (Not value Is Nothing) Then
            value.People.Add(Me)
         End If
      End If
```

```
        End Set
    End Property

    ' Fields
    Private _firstName As String
    Private _ID As Integer
    Private _IDRole As Integer
    Private _lastName As String
    Private _Role As EntityRef(Of Role)
End Class
```

In the Set accessor we check if the value specified is different from the one within the Entity property of the _Role field. If so, we have to remove the old one before adding the new value. Finally, the Person object pointed by the Me keyword is added to the People collection to maintain referential integrity:

```
    Public Property Role() As Role
        Get
            Return Me._Role.Entity
        End Get
        Set(ByVal value As Role)
            Dim role1 As Role = Me._Role.Entity
            If (Not role1 Is value) Then
                If (Not role1 Is Nothing) Then
                    Me._Role.Entity = Nothing
                    role1.People.Remove(Me)
                End If
                Me._Role.Entity = value
                If (Not value Is Nothing) Then
                    value.People.Add(Me)
                End If
            End If
        End Set
    End Property
```

Using Two Related Entity Classes

Now that we've defined the relationship between two entity classes we can use it to query and modify data.

The code in Listing 2-10 retrieves a single Person object and then uses its role.

Listing 2-10. Retrieving a Person and Using Its Role Property

```
    Dim people = New PeopleDataContext()

    people.Log = Console.Out
```

```
Dim query = From p In people.People _
    Where p.ID = 1 _
    Select p

For Each Dim row In query
    Console.WriteLine( _
        "Full Name: {0} {1} Role: {2}", _
        row.FirstName, _
        row.LastName, _
        row.Role.RoleDescription)

Next
```

We don't need to the join the two tables to access the role. LINQ to SQL generates two SQL queries to retrieve both the Person and related Role data. See the two SQL statements in Figure 2-7.

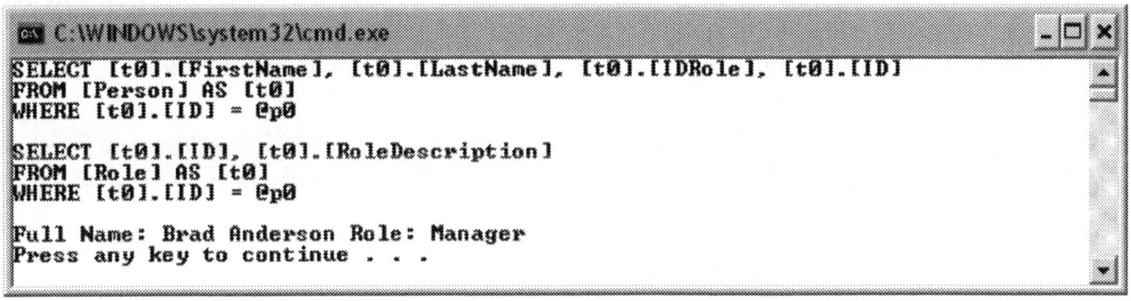

Figure 2-7. The output of Listing 2-10

Note in Figure 2-7 that the @p0 parameter is used in both the queries. They are two different queries, so the @p0 parameter has different values. The @p0 parameter used in the first query is the value specified in the LINQ query. The @p0 parameter used in the second query is the value specified with the ThisKey property of the Association attribute used in the Role property decoration.

In Listing 2-11 we'll retrieve a role and then use its People property to add a new person.

Listing 2-11. Adding a New Person to the Database Starting from a Role

```
Public Class AddExample
    Public Shared Function whereCondition(ByVal p As Role) As Boolean
        Return p.ID = 1
    End Function

    Sub Listing2_11()
        Dim people = New PeopleDataContext()
        Dim predicateDelegate As New Func(Of Role, Boolean)(AddressOf whereCondition)
```

```
        people.Log = Console.Out

        Dim role = people.Roles.Single(predicateDelegate)

        Dim person As New Person()
        person.FirstName = "From"
        person.LastName = "Relationship"
        role.People.Add(person)

        people.SubmitChanges()

    End Sub
End Class
```

Since there's a relationship between the two entity classes, we don't have to specify the IDRole for the Person object. It will be assigned by the Attach_Person delegate function when a new Person object is added to the people collection of the Role entity class. Figure 2-8 shows the INSERT statement generated by LINQ to SQL. Note that a local transaction is automatically created for the INSERT.

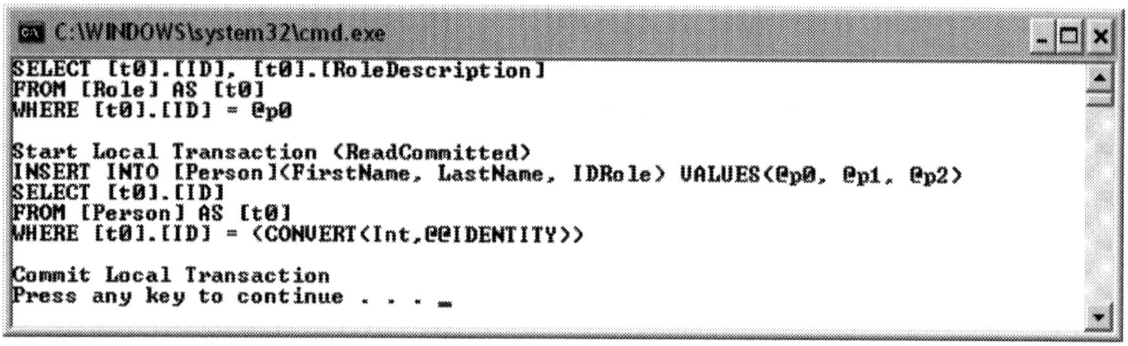

Figure 2-8. The INSERT statement generated by LINQ to SQL

Deleting a row and every row related to it is really simple when a relationship is defined between two entity classes. Listing 2-12 deletes a role and all its related Person records.

Listing 2-12. Deleting a Role and All of Its Related Person Records

```
Public Class DeleteExample
    Public Shared newID As Integer

    Public Shared Function whereCondition(ByVal p As Role) As Boolean
        Return p.ID = newID
    End Function
```

```
Sub Listing2_12()
    Dim people = New PeopleDataContext()
    Dim predicateDelegate As New Func(Of Role, Boolean)(AddressOf whereCondition)

    people.Log = Console.Out

    Dim role As New Role()
    role.RoleDescription = "Administrator"

    Dim person As New Person()
    person.FirstName = "From"
    person.LastName = "Code"

    role.People.Add(person)
    people.Roles.Add(role)

    people.SubmitChanges()

    newID = role.ID

    Dim admin = people.Roles.Single(predicateDelegate)
    people.Roles.Remove(admin)
    people.SubmitChanges()
End Sub
End Class
```

It creates a new role as follows:

```
Dim role As New Role()
role.RoleDescription = "Administrator"
```

It then adds a new person to it:

```
Dim person As New Person()
person.FirstName = "From"
person.LastName = "Code"

role.People.Add(person)
people.Roles.Add(role)
```

The code uses the new role's identifier to retrieve the new row added to the database:

```
Dim admin = people.Roles.Single(predicateDelegate)
people.Roles.Remove(admin)
people.SubmitChanges()
```

This behavior is not obtained by the Association attribute and its properties. No reflection technique is used to infer the rows related to the Role entity object. Moreover, there is no check on foreign key constraint rules, such as deleting each related row in a cascade. The secret is in the EntitySet(Of T) constructor. We have provided two delegate functions responding to the Add and the Remove events of the Person entity class. In the body of the Detach_Person delegate function we have set the Role value to Nothing, raising a call to the Set accessor of the Role property. It's in the body of Detach_Person that you will find the Remove() method of the Person row related to the role. The Remove() method applied by the parent class will call the Detach delegate function for each child row related to it. This process will be performed once for each Person object related to the Role object.

Other LINQ to SQL Features

In this section we'll cover the following:

- Using SQLMetal to produce entity classes and associations automatically
- Using the INotifyPropertyChanging interface to communicate with LINQ about changes
- Using the optimistic concurrency and database transactions
- Using stored procedures
- Creating a database from a program

SQLMetal

LINQ to SQL has a command-line tool called SQLMetal that generates entity classes, properties, and associations automatically. Table 2-3 lists the SQLMetal options.

Table 2-3. SQLMetal Generation Tool Options

Option	Description
/server:<name>	Represents the Microsoft SQL Server server name to which the SQLMetal tool connects.
/database:<name>	Represents the Microsoft SQL Server database name to use to produce entity classes.
/user:<name>	Represents the user's name to use to connect to the database server.
/password:<name>	Represents the user's password to use to connect to the database server.
/views	Obtains the database views extraction.

Option	Description
/functions	Obtains the database user functions extraction.
/sprocs	Obtains the database stored procedures extraction.
/code:<filename>	Lets you specify the name of the file that will contain the entity classes and data context.
/language:<name>	There are two options: C# (the default) and VB. Use one of these options to produce a file in the specified language.
/xml:<filename>	Lets you specify an XML filename that will contain the database metadata and some information about classes and properties.
/map:<filename>	Obtains an external XML file with mapping attributes. The entities produced in the code will not contain class and property attributes' decorations because they have been included in the XML mapping file.
/pluralize	Obtains entity class and property names with English plural.
/namespace	Lets you specify the namespace that will contain the generated entity classes.
/dataAttributes	Lets you add attributes to entity class properties, such as the Precision attribute for numeric values and DataObjectField to provide information about the schema of the underlying data.
/timeout:<value>	Lets you specify the timeout (in seconds) to use for each database command.

The following command uses SQLMetal to generate the entity classes to access to the People database within a Microsoft SQL Server 2005 database using Windows Integrated Security:

```
sqlmetal /server:pc-ferracchiati /database:People /pluralize /language:vb /code:People.vb
```

If you want to use SQL Server security you have to add two more options to the command, specifying username and password:

sqlmetal /server:pc-ferracchiati /database:People /user:sa /password:sapass /pluralize /language:vb /code:People.vb

You can also generate entity classes simply by specifying a database's data (.MDF) file:

sqlmetal /pluralize /language:vb /code:People.vb c:\data\people.mdf

---

Note ➤ If you use spaces after the colon that separates options from values, you will receive an unhandled exception.

The INotifyPropertyChanging Interface

By opening up the code produced by the SQLMetal tool, we can see some minor differences between it and the code we wrote. There are four types of constructor accepting different connection attributes, such as a connection string and an IDBConnection object, but the big difference is the use of INotifyPropertyChanging and INotifyPropertyChanged:

```
<Table(Name:="Person")> _
Partial Public Class Person
  Implements System.Data.DLinq.INotifyPropertyChanging, _
    System.ComponentModel.INotifyPropertyChanged

  Private _ID As Integer
```

The INotifyPropertyChanging interface is in the System.Data.DLinq namespace. The INotifyPropertyChanged interface is in the System.ComponentModel namespace. Both interfaces require two events:

```
Public Event PropertyChanging As PropertyChangedEventHandler _
  Implements INotifyPropertyChanging.PropertyChanging

Public Event PropertyChanged As PropertyChangedEventHandler _
  Implements INotifyPropertyChanged.PropertyChanged
```

They also require virtual methods to handle the interfaces:

```
Protected Overridable Sub OnPropertyChanging(ByVal PropertyName As String)
  If ((Me.PropertyChangingEvent Is Nothing) _
      = false) Then
    RaiseEvent PropertyChanging(Me, New PropertyChangedEventArgs(PropertyName))
  End If
End Sub

Protected Overridable Sub OnPropertyChanged(ByVal PropertyName As String)
```

```
If ((Me.PropertyChangedEvent Is Nothing) _
      = false) Then
   RaiseEvent PropertyChanged(Me, New PropertyChangedEventArgs(PropertyName))
   End If
End Sub
```

In the generated code, each Set accessor of a column calls two methods. The OnPropertyChanging method is called just before the variable is set to the provided value. The OnPropertyChanged method is called just after the variable is set.

```
<Column(Storage:="_ID", DBType:="Int NOT NULL IDENTITY", Id:=true, AutoGen:=true)> _
   Public Property ID() As Integer
      Get
         Return Me._ID
      End Get
      Set
         If ((Me._ID = value) _
            = false) Then
            Me.OnPropertyChanging("ID")
            Me._ID = value
            Me.OnPropertyChanged("ID")
         End If
      End Set
   End Property
```

The use of INotifyPropertyChanging and INotifyPropertyChanged is not mandatory. In fact, the code we wrote works very well. But these interfaces help LINQ change tracking. The OnPropertyChanging and OnPropertyChanged methods significantly improve change tracking because LINQ doesn't have to check changes manually. If you don't use these two interfaces and you don't inform LINQ about row changes, it will use two copies of the same object to understand if something is changed. There will be two objects representing each table, wasting memory and cycles when you call SubmitChanges().

Optimistic Concurrency and Database Transactions

What we have done to this point works well only if we are the only ones working on a set of data. If an application uses a LINQ query to retrieve data from a table already accessed by another user and then it tries to modify some rows, it could get an exception. This is because LINQ to SQL uses *optimistic concurrency.*

LINQ to SQL tracks changes to our objects after they are retrieved by a query and filled by a For Each statement or a call to a caching method such as ToList(). If another user has retrieved a row from the database and already changed its contents, when we try to submit our changes we'll get an exception. In fact, LINQ's change-tracking service discovers that the row has been changed from its original state (as of when we retrieved it) and raises the exception. To test the optimistic concurrency feature, write and execute the code in Listing 2-13.

Listing 2-13. Testing the Optimistic Concurrency Feature

```
Public Class OptimisticConcurrencyExample
    Public Shared Function whereCondition(ByVal p As Person) As Boolean
        Return p.ID = 1
    End Function

    Sub Listing2_13()
        Dim people = New PeopleDataContext()
        Dim predicateDelegate As New Func(Of Person, Boolean)(AddressOf whereCondition)

        Dim person = people.People.Single(predicateDelegate)

        person.FirstName = "Optimistic"
        person.LastName = "Concurrency"

        Console.ReadLine()

        people.SubmitChanges()
    End Sub
End Class
```

The code simply retrieves the Person row whose identifier is equal to 1, changes some attributes, and submits the changes after a key is pressed. This allows us to execute another instance of the same application that retrieves the same row before we press a key in the other instance of the application. Pressing a key in the first application will modify the row, whereas pressing a key in the second application will cause the exception shown in Figure 2-9.

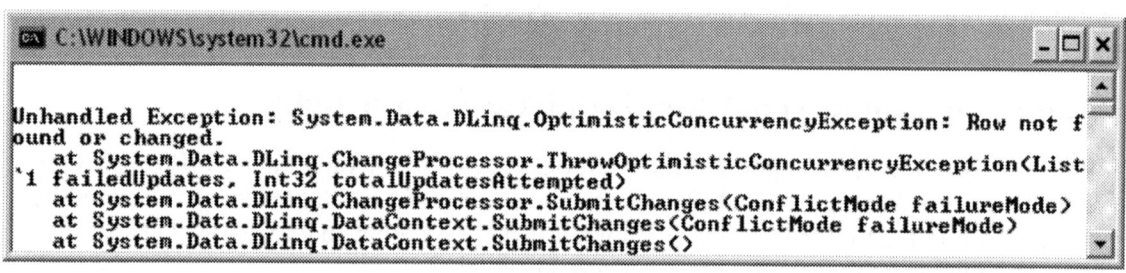

Figure 2-9. The exception thrown by LINQ when the optimistic concurrency is violated

Concurrency is managed by the DataContext class. When we call SubmitChanges(), the data context creates a local transaction using the ReadCommit isolation level; that is, using optimistic concurrency.

This is the default. When we decorate the properties of the entity classes we can indicate which of them participate in optimistic concurrency. Using the UpdateCheck property of the Column attribute we can specify Never and LINQ will ignore the column during concurrency checking.

```
<Column(Name:="FirstName", Storage:="_firstName", _
        DbType:="nvarchar NOT NULL", _
        UpdateCheck:=UpdateCheck.Never)> _
Public Property FirstName() As String
   Get
      Return Me._firstName
   End Get
   Set(ByVal value As String)
      Me._firstName = value
   End Set
End Property

<Column(Name:="LastName", Storage:="_lastName", _
        DbType:="nvarchar NOT NULL", _
        UpdateCheck:=UpdateCheck.Never)> _
Public Property LastName() As String
   Get
      Return Me._lastName
   End Get
   Set(ByVal value As String)
      Me._lastName = value
   End Set
End Property
```

After we modify the Person entity class as shown, the code in Listing 2-13 will work without exceptions because the two columns don't participate in optimistic concurrency checking.

LINQ to SQL provides an advanced technique to manage update conflicts. When we call SubmitChanges(), we can specify a ConflictMode enum value to change the way optimistic concurrency is managed by LINQ.

Using ConflictMode.ContinueOnConflict the OptimisticConcurrencyException is filled with some attributes that we can use to personalize the way optimistic concurrency is managed. Using a Try statement we can catch the OptimisticConcurrencyException then use its Resolve() method to specify one of three values that in turn specify three different way to resolve update conflicts:

KeepChanges: The old values contained in the object are refreshed with the new values changed by the other client. A new SubmitChanges() call is executed automatically and the current values within the object are used to update the row.

KeepCurrentValues: This rolls back each change made by the other client to the original database state. A new SubmitChanges() call is executed automatically and the current values within the object are used to update the row.

OverwriteCurrentValues: The object replaces its data with the new state of the row in the database.

The code in Listing 2-14 calls the Resolve method with KeepChanges after an optimistic concurrency exception has been detected.

Listing 2-14. A Try Statement to Manage Optimistic Concurrency Conflict

```
Public Class OptimisticConcurrencyExample2
    Public Shared Function whereCondition(ByVal p As Person) As Boolean
        Return p.ID = 1
    End Function

    Sub Listing2_14()
        Dim people = New PeopleDataContext()
        Dim predicateDelegate As New Func(Of Person, Boolean)(AddressOf whereCondition)

        Dim person = people.People.Single(predicateDelegate)

        person.FirstName = "Optimistic"
        person.LastName = "Concurrency"

        Try
            people.SubmitChanges(ConflictMode.ContinueOnConflict)
        Catch oce As OptimisticConcurrencyException
            oce.Resolve(RefreshMode.KeepChanges)
        End Try
    End Sub
End Class
```

Sometimes we need to lock a row until we've finished managing it. This can be done by using a transaction and the *pessimistic concurrency* feature.

.NET 2.0 provides the TransactionScope class in the System.Transactions namespace. A simple way to implement pessimistic concurrency is with a using statement. Within a Using block we can instantiate a TransactionScope and, as the last operation, call its Complete() method (see Listing 2-15)

Listing 2-15. Implementing Pessimistic Concurrency with TransactionScope

```
Public Class TransactionExample
    Public Shared Function whereCondition(ByVal p As Person) As Boolean
        Return p.ID = 1
    End Function
```

```
Sub Listing2_15()
    Dim people = New PeopleDataContext()
    Dim predicateDelegate As New Func(Of Person, Boolean)(AddressOf whereCondition)

    Using t As New TransactionScope()
        Dim person = people.People.Single(predicateDelegate)

        person.FirstName = "Optimistic"
        person.LastName = "Concurrency"

        Console.ReadLine()

        people.SubmitChanges()

        t.Complete()
    End Using
End Sub
End Class
```

We can test the pessimistic concurrency by executing two separate application instances (like in Listing 2-13). Both transactions attempt to lock the same row, and SQL Server decides which one (the "deadlock victim") to terminate (see Figure 2-10).

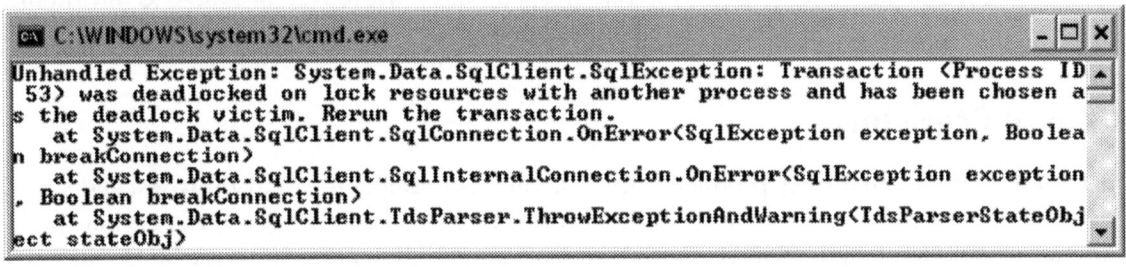

Figure 2-10. Pessimistic concurrency deadlock resolution

LINQ to SQL is able to integrate itself even with the old ADO.NET application code. We can use the DataContext class with SqlTransaction classes, but we'll have to do much more work to implement the local transaction. In the code snippet in Listing 2-16 a new Role is added to the related table using an ADO.NET local transaction.

Listing 2-16. Using an ADO.NET Local Transaction with LINQ to SQL

```
Dim people As New PeopleDataContext()
people.Log = Console.Out

Dim r As New Role()
r.RoleDescription = "Integration with old ADO.NET apps"
```

```
      people.Roles.Add(r)

      people.Connection.Open()
      people.LocalTransaction = people.Connection.BeginTransaction()

      Try
         people.SubmitChanges()
         people.LocalTransaction.Commit()
         people.AcceptChanges()
      Catch ex As Exception
         people.LocalTransaction.Rollback()
         people.RejectChanges()
         Throw ex
      Finally
         If people.Connection.State = System.Data.ConnectionState.Open Then
            people.Connection.Close()
         End If

         people.LocalTransaction = Nothing
      End Try
```

As you can see in Listing 2-16, we have to pay attention to some things, such as manually opening and closing the connection and calling Commit() or Rollback() (when everything is fine or something goes wrong, respectively). Moreover, we have to inform the DataContext class to accept or to reject changes appropriately.

Stored Procedures

LINQ to SQL automatically produces SQL statements to select rows, insert rows, and so on. We often prefer to use existing stored procedures or create new ones to access data and improve application performance. *Stored procedures* are SQL statement procedures that are precompiled and stored within the SQL Server database. When you call a stored procedure, the database server simply executes it without doing other operations such as checking SQL syntax within it. In many cases calling a stored procedure to retrieve rows works better than using dynamic SQL.

LINQ to SQL provides the ExecuteCommand method of the DataContext class to call stored procedures. This method has two parameters: the SQL command to execute and the collection of parameters that can be used in the SQL command.

Within the class inheriting from the DataContext we can add a method to call the ExecuteCommand() method that provides the stored procedure name and its parameters:

```
Public Sub InsertRole(ByVal r As Role)
   MyBase.ExecuteCommand("exec uspInsertRole @description={0}", r.RoleDescription)
End Sub
```

The uspInsertRole stored procedure simply adds a new role, accepting its description as a parameter (Role's identifier is auto-incremented by the server since it is of the identity type). The ExecuteCommand() method will substitute each placeholder specified in the command with the related parameter contained in the collection.

This is not still sufficient, however; we have to tell LINQ to SQL to use this new method when a new role has to be added to the database. We can accomplish this by specifying the InsertMethod attribute before the method declaration:

```
<InsertMethod()> _
Public Sub InsertRole(ByVal r As Role)
    MyBase.ExecuteCommand("exec uspInsertRole @description={0}", r.RoleDescription)
End Sub
```

Up to this point we have written all the necessary code to execute our stored procedure instead of executing the code generated by LINQ to SQL. In Listing 2-17 a new role is added to the related table and the Log property is used to show the code called by LINQ.

Listing 2-17. A New Role Is Added and the Stored Procedure Is Called Automatically.

```
Dim people As New PeopleDataContext()
people.Log = Console.Out

Dim r As New Role()
r.RoleDescription = "By SP"
people.Roles.Add(r)

people.SubmitChanges()
```

When you're executing the code you will obtain the result shown in Figure 2-11, which displays how LINQ calls the stored procedure automatically.

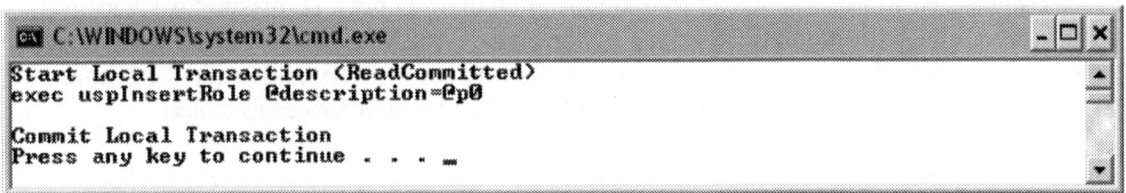

Figure 2-11. The framework uses our stored procedure instead of generating the code to insert a new role.

To update rows using a stored procedure we can specify an update method in the class that inherits from the DataContext class, and decorate it with the UpdateMethod attribute. The prototype of the update method is a bit different from the rest because it has to accept two parameters: the former is the object to update in its original state, and the latter is the object to update in its current state. We have to check each condition manually before calling the ExecuteCommand() method. For example, in the following code snippet, before the stored procedure is executed the role description is compared to the original one to discover if it is really changed:

```
<UpdateMethod()> _
Public Sub UpdateRole(ByVal oldRole As Role, ByVal newRole As Role)
    If (Not oldRole.RoleDescription Is newRole.RoleDescription) Then
        Dim iRowsAffected As Integer = _
            MyBase.ExecuteCommand("exec uspUpdateRole @id={0}, _
                                             @description={1}", _
                                             newRole.ID, _
                                             newRole.RoleDescription)

        If (iRowsAffected < 1) Then
            Throw New OptimisticConcurrencyException
        End If
    End If
End Sub
```

Moreover, we have to check the return value of ExecuteCommand() because if it is less than 1 an optimistic concurrency error has occurred. In that case we must throw a new OptimisticConcurrencyException exception.

Note ➤ If you declare an update method with just one parameter and you decorate it with UpdateMethod you will not receive a compiler error, but the method will not be called.

You may be wondering why a role identifier changing check is missing; it's because this kind of check is automatically done by the change-tracking service. So if in the code snippet in Listing 2-18, after having retrieved the role row you try to modify the primary key identifier value you will obtain an exception when SubmitChanges()is called.

Listing 2-18. Updating a Role Calling a Stored Procedure Instead of Using the LINQ to SQL Update-Generated Statement

```
Public Class UpdateBySPExample
    Public Shared Function whereCondition(ByVal r As Role) As Boolean
        Return r.ID = 1
    End Function

    Sub Listing2_18()
        Dim people = New PeopleDataContext()
        Dim predicateDelegate As New Func(Of Role, Boolean)(AddressOf whereCondition)
```

```
people.Log = Console.Out

Dim role = people.Roles.Single(predicateDelegate)
role.RoleDescription = "By Update stored procedure"

people.SubmitChanges()

    End Sub
End Class
```

To delete a row by using a stored procedure we have to add a new method in the class that inherits from the DataContext class and decorate it with the DeleteMethod attribute:

```
<DeleteMethod()> _
Public Sub DeleteRole(ByVal r As Role)
    MyBase.ExecuteCommand("exec uspDeleteRole @id={0}", r.ID)
End Sub
```

In this way the code in Listing 2-19 will call a stored procedure to remove each role from the database.

Listing 2-19. Using a Stored Procedure Instead of an Autogenerated Delete Statement to Delete All the Roles That Have a Particular Description

```
Dim people As New PeopleDataContext()
people.Log = Console.Out

Dim query = From r In people.Roles _
    Where r.RoleDescription = "By SP" _
    Select r

For Each Dim r As Role In query
    people.Roles.Remove(r)
Next

people.SubmitChanges()
```

LINQ to SQL doesn't provide an attribute to decorate stored procedures that return rows. However, by using SQLMetal with the /sprocs option we can generate entity classes containing methods that have the same name as a stored procedure. Based on the syntax of the stored procedure, the generated code could return a single value or a collection of objects.

The simplest case is a stored procedure that computes scalar operations using the COUNT operator:

```
create procedure uspCountPerson
```

as

```
        declare @count int
        set @count = (select count(ID) from person)
        return @count
```

Executing the SQLMetal application with the /sprocs option, the generated code will contain the following method:

```
<StoredProcedure(Name:="uspCountPerson")> _
Public Function UspCountPerson() As Integer
    Dim info As MethodInfo = MethodBase.GetCurrentMethod
    Dim result As StoredProcedureResult = MyBase.ExecuteStoredProcedure(info)
    Return result.ReturnValue.Value
End Function
```

The method will be decorated with the StoredProcedure attribute where the stored procedure name will be specified. The method name will be similar or equal to the stored procedure name. SQLMetal will infer the method return type by analyzing the SQL statement that the stored procedure uses. For this reason there are some situations the SQLMetal tool can't handle. If the stored procedure uses temporary tables or dynamic SQL (by calling the sp_executesql system-stored procedure), the tool will not be able to infer the result's type. Therefore, it will not able to define a related method with a valid return type. These kinds of stored procedures cannot be used with LINQ to SQL. Finally, the body of the generated method contains a call to the ExecuteStoredProcedure method provided by the DataContext class. This method has two parameters indicating the MethodInfo object for the current method (useful for discovering the stored procedure name by reflection) and a collection of parameters that have to be passed to the stored procedure. Listing 2-20 uses this method to call the related stored procedure.

Listing 2-20. Using the Method Associated with a Stored Procedure to Retrieve the Number of Person Rows in the Database

```
    Dim people As New PeopleDataContext()

    Console.WriteLine("Person count = {0}", people.UspCountPerson())
```

If we have a stored procedure selecting a set of rows, we can use the same technique to produce a method, calling that stored procedure and returning a collection of objects:

```
create procedure uspGetRoleDescription
        @description       varchar(50)
as
        SELECT       ID, RoleDescription
        FROM  Role
        WHERE        RoleDescription LIKE @description
```

The stored procedure in the example returns a set of role rows in which the role description is like a provided parameter. Since the selected columns have been specified in the Role class we can define a method that calls this stored procedure and returns a collection of Role objects.

```
<StoredProcedure(Name:="uspGetRoleDescription")> _
Public Function UspGetRoleDescription( _
    <Parameter(DbType:="VarChar(50)")> ByVal description As String) _
        As StoredProcedureResult(Of Role)
    Return MyBase.ExecuteStoredProcedure(Of Role)(MethodBase.GetCurrentMethod, _
                                                    description)
End Function
```

When the stored procedure accepts parameters, we have to decorate each related method parameter with the Parameter attribute where we specify the database data type. The ExecuteStoredProcedure(Of T) method uses the properties contained in the class specified as parameter T to fill the object with the column value returned by the stored procedure. If the stored procedure returns data that is not mapped to any class within your code, the SQLMetal tool will create a new class to contain the result of the stored procedure call.

Note ➤ SQLMetal is not able to understand if the stored procedure returns values that fit an existing class. It will always generate a new class to contain them.

Listing 2-21 shows the code that calls this method.

Listing 2-21. Using the UspGetRoleDescription Method to Retrieve Roles Rows

```
Dim people As New PeopleDataContext()

For Each Dim r As Role In people.UspGetRoleDescription("M%")
    Console.WriteLine("Role: {0} {1}", r.ID.ToString(), _
            r.RoleDescription)
Next
```

When the stored procedure contains more than one SELECT statement, the method generated by the SQLMetal will return multiple result sets. In the following example a stored procedure contains two SELECT statements to retrieve person and role rows.

```
create procedure uspGetRolesAndPeople
as
        SELECT * FROM Person
        SELECT * FROM Role
```

By executing the SQLMetal tool to generate code for the new stored procedure, we will obtain the following method:

```
<StoredProcedure(Name:="uspGetRolesAndPeople")> _
Public Function UspGetRolesAndPeople() As StoredProcedureMultipleResult
    Return MyBase.ExecuteStoredProcedure(MethodBase.GetCurrentMethod)
End Function
```

The StoredProcedureMultipleResult return type contains the GetResults(Of T) method to differentiate the two result sets by simply providing the class type we want to retrieve. Listing 2-22 shows the method's usage.

Listing 2-22. Using the Stored Procedure Method to Return Multiple Results

```
Dim people As New PeopleDataContext()

Dim results As StoredProcedureMultipleResult = people.UspGetRolesAndPeople()

Dim query = From p In results.GetResults(Of Person)(), r In results.GetResults(Of Role)() _
    Where p.IDRole = r.ID AndAlso p.ID = 1 _
    Select New {p.FirstName, p.LastName, r.RoleDescription}

For Each Dim row In query
    Console.WriteLine("Person: {0} {1} - Role: {2}", row.FirstName, _
        row.LastName, _
        row.RoleDescription)
Next
```

First we have to call the method to retrieve the multiple results and store them into the StoredProcedureMultipleResult object. Then we can use it as usual to query rows based on conditions. The GetResults(Of T) class is used to retrieve person or role rows by specifying the related class type as a T parameter.

The last case supported by LINQ to SQL is for stored procedures using OUTPUT parameters:

```
create procedure uspGetTotalSalaryAmountPerYear
    @year    int,
    @amount        money output
as
    set @amount = ( select sum(SalaryYear)
                            from Salary
                            where year=@year)
    select @amount
```

The stored procedure above computes the total money amount for the salary in a specified year. When the SQLMetal tool encounters this stored procedure it will produce the following method:

```
<StoredProcedure(Name:="uspGetTotalSalaryAmountPerYear")> _
Public Function UspGetTotalSalaryAmountPerYear( _
    <Parameter(DbType:="Int")> ByVal year As Nullable(Of Integer), _
    <Parameter(DbType:="Money")> ByRef amount As Nullable(Of Decimal)) _
        As Integer
    Dim info As MethodInfo = MethodBase.GetCurrentMethod
    Dim result As StoredProcedureResult = _
        MyBase.ExecuteStoredProcedure(info, year, amount)
    amount = result.GetParameterValue(1)
    Return result.ReturnValue.Value
End Function
```

First the OUTPUT parameter is transformed into a *ref* method parameter. Then the StoredProcedureResult is used with GetParameterValue() to set the value of the ByRef variable.

Note ➤ The code generated by the SQLMetal tool is still not perfect because the application is not able to infer all method code for all SQL statements. For the stored procedure analyzed in the preceding code sample it adds useless code such as System.Nullable parameters even when the column doesn't accept null values, or a new class to contain a return value even if the SQL statement doesn't select any rows.

Listing 2-23 shows the code necessary to execute this method and retrieve the total money amount for the year 2004.

Listing 2-23. Using the Method Related to the Stored Procedure to Retrieve the Total Money Amount for the Year 2004

```
Dim people As New PeopleDataContext()

Dim total As Nullable(Of Decimal) = 0
Dim year As Integer = 2004

people.UspGetTotalSalaryAmountPerYear(year, total)

Console.WriteLine(total.ToString())
```

User-Defined Functions

LINQ to SQL also supports *user-defined functions* (UDFs), which return both scalar values and result sets.

Using the SQLMetal tool's /functions option, we can obtain a new method in the class that inherits from the DataContext class; the new method is decorated with attributes for building a SQL statement that calls a UDF.

The following UDF returns the initials of the person whose identifier is specified as an argument:

```
create function udfGetInitials(@id    int)
returns varchar(2)
as
begin
         declare @initials varchar(2)
         set @initials = (SELECT LEFT(FirstName,1) + LEFT(LastName,1)
                                       FROM Person
                                       WHERE ID = @id)

         return @initials
end
```

Executing the SQLMetal tool to generate entity classes and user-defined function code, we obtain the following method code:

```
<[Function](Name:="[dbo].[udfGetInitials]")> _
Public Function UdfGetInitials(ByVal id As Nullable(Of Integer)) As String
    Dim info As MethodInfo = MethodInfo.GetCurrentMethod()
    Dim mc As MethodCallExpression = expression.Call(info, _
                    expression.Constant(Me), _
                    New Expression() {expression.Constant(id, _
                    GetType(Nullable(Of Integer)))})
    Return Sequence.Single(Of String)(MyBase.CreateQuery(Of String)(mc))
End Function
```

First the Function attribute is used to decorate the method and inform LINQ that it is associated with the UDF specified with the Name parameter.

Then in the body of the method a MethodCallExpression is built, but the execution of the UDF is left to the DataContext class with the CreateQuery() method. The UdfGetInitials method leaves the execution of the UDF to the DataContext class. CreateQuery() takes the MethodCallExpression object and creates the query. This feature can handle both standard and inline UDF calls.

Listing 2-24 shows a code snippet in which the UDF is called within a LINQ query to obtain the initials of each person present in the Person table.

Listing 2-24. The UDF Is Transformed into a Method That Can be Called as Usual from Our Code.

```
Dim people As New PeopleDataContext()

people.Log = Console.Out
```

```
Dim query = From p In people.People _
    Select New {p.ID, Initials := people.UdfGetInitials(p.ID)}

For Each Dim row In query
    Console.WriteLine("PersonID: {0} - Initials: {1}", row.ID, row.Initials)
Next
```

Figure 2-12 shows the output from Listing 2-24.

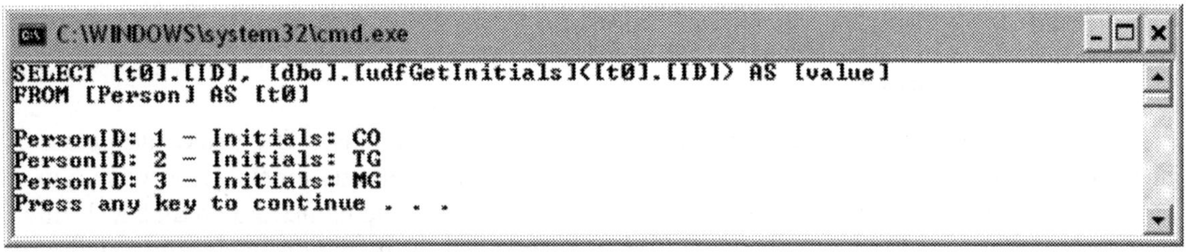

Figure 2-12. The output shows how the UDF calculates the person's initials.

As Figure 2-12 shows, the SELECT statement built by LINQ contains an inline call to the UDF. That's because we have used the related method within our LINQ query. If we use the method outside a query we will obtain a simple statement like this one:

SELECT dbo.udfGetInitials(@p0)

Database Creation

Since Microsoft has released a free version of Microsoft SQL Server 2005 called Express Edition, we can easily create an application that stores data using a database instead of XML files or some other data storage. In fact, SQL Server Express Edition can be distributed without limits, allowing us to install and use it even with desktop client applications. Focusing on that feature, a way to create a database on the fly could be really useful.

LINQ to SQL provides a method of the DataContext class called CreateDatabase. Using the attributes specified in the entity classes, where each column is decorated with options such as column name, column database data type, and so on, LINQ is able to create a new database.

Note ➤ When you need to create a database from scratch using the CreateDatabase method you must use the DBType option for each column. LINQ uses this information to create the column data type.

Listing 2-25 shows how you can use CreateDatabase() to create a new database.

Listing 2-25. Creating a New Database with the CreateDatabase() Method

```
Dim people = New PeopleDataContext( _
    "Data Source=.;Initial Catalog=PeopleFromCode;Integrated Security=True")

If people.DatabaseExists() Then
    people.DeleteDatabase()
End If

people.CreateDatabase()
```

Note the connection string that points to a nonexistent database. The DataContext class uses the connection string to discover whether the database already exists. Otherwise it uses the catalog option specified in the connection string as database name and creates it. Using the DatabaseExists and DeleteDatabase methods we can check if the database already exists and if so, drop it.

There are some limitations when using the CreateDatabase method to create a database:

- Because stored procedures, UDFs, and triggers are not defined in the entity classes as structure, they are not reproduced.

- Despite the fact that associations could be declared into entity classes, the method is not able to create foreign keys and constraints.

- The application must impersonate a user who has rights to create the database.

LINQ to SQL in Visual Studio 2005

In conjunction with the LINQ May 2006 CTP release, Visual Studio 2005 provides functionality to support LINQ application development. Some templates are added to the New Project and the New Web Site windows (see Figure 2-13). The compiler is upgraded to support LINQ query syntax, and IntelliSense will support almost every LINQ component. Further, a really great tool has been added to Visual Studio: the DLinq Designer. It is similar to SQLMetal in that it produces the code to manage entity classes related to database tables, but it has these advantages:

- It produces entity classes just for specified tables, not for the full database.

- It produces entity-class associations using a visual tool.

- It supports entity-class hierarchies.

- It is a visual tool and the final result offers a visual representation of classes, associations, and so on within a colored diagram.

A DLinq Designer Example

Using DLinq Designer is very easy. Starting from a LINQ Preview project such as a LINQ Windows application, you have to add a new DLinqObjects item to the solution. Visual Studio then shows you the DLinq Designer together with a new toolbox.

Follow these steps to add database support using DLinq Designer:

1. Launch Visual Studio 2005 and create a new project with File ➤ New Project... .

2. Choose the LINQ Windows Application template, as shown in Figure 2-13.

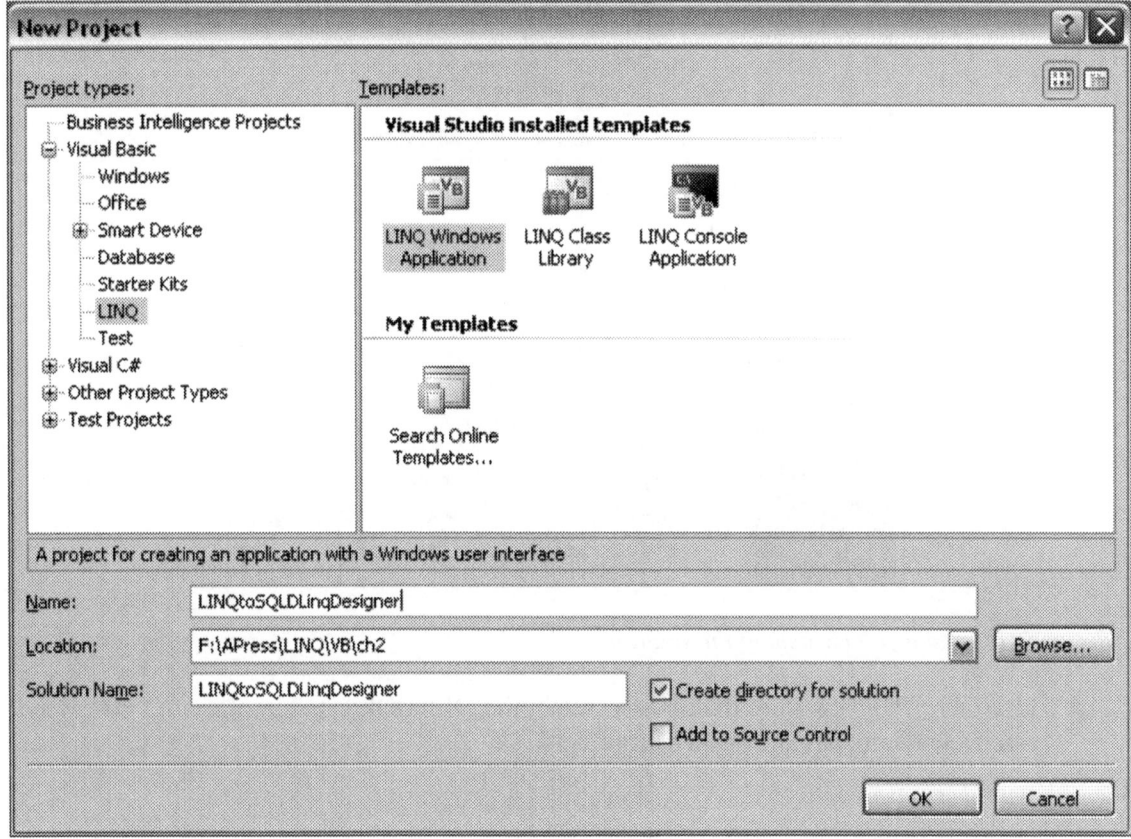

Figure 2-13. Creating a new LINQ Windows application from Visual Studio

3. From the Solution Explorer, right-click on the solution name and choose Add ➤ New Item from the context menu as shown in Figure 2-14.

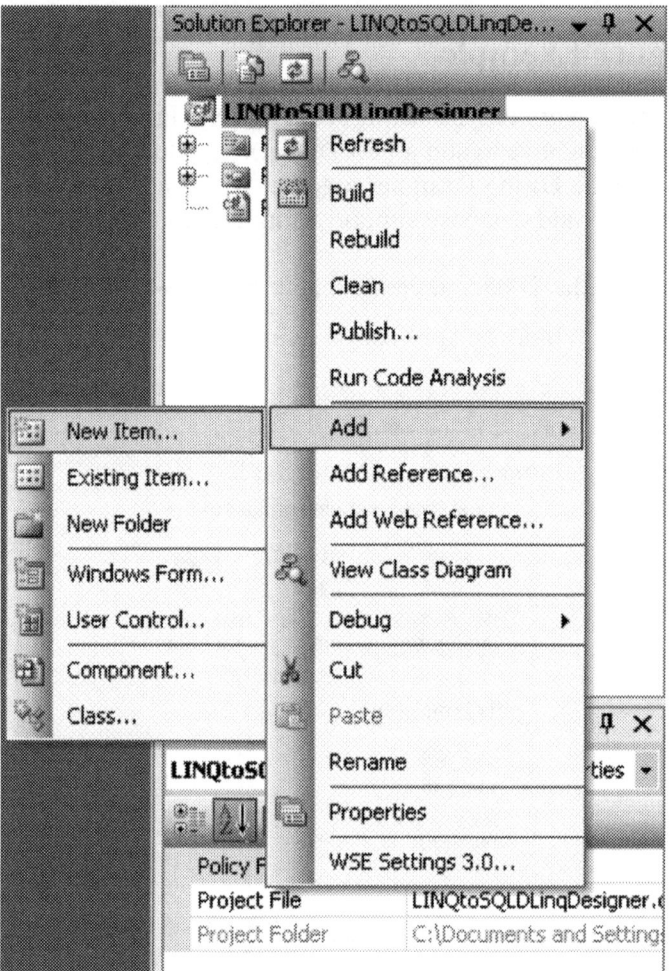

Figure 2-14. Adding a new item to the solution

4. From the Add New Item dialog box, select the DLinqObjects template and give it a significant name, as shown in Figure 2-15.

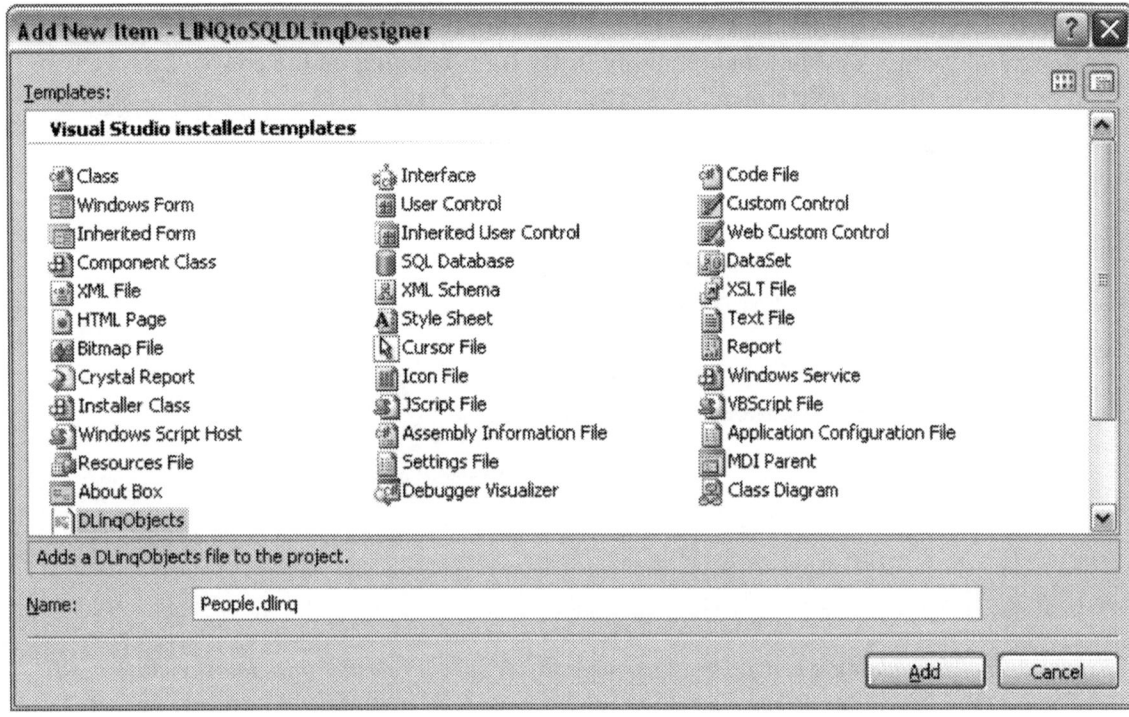

Figure 2-15. Adding a new DLinqObjects template to the solution

5. At this point Visual Studio will present the DLinq Designer and provide a new toolbox section (see Figure 2-16). You can use the new toolbox to graphically specify your table's structure.

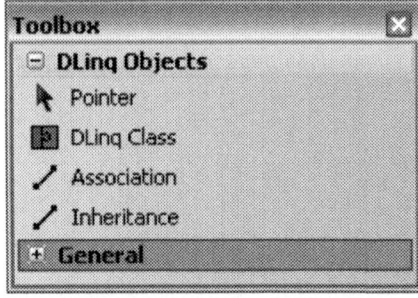

Figure 2-16. The new DLinq Objects toolbox provided by the DLinq Designer

Double-click on the DLinq Class item; a new empty entity class is added to the designer, allowing us to start manipulating it. By right-clicking on the entity class we can add new properties or delete them, as shown in Figure 2-17.

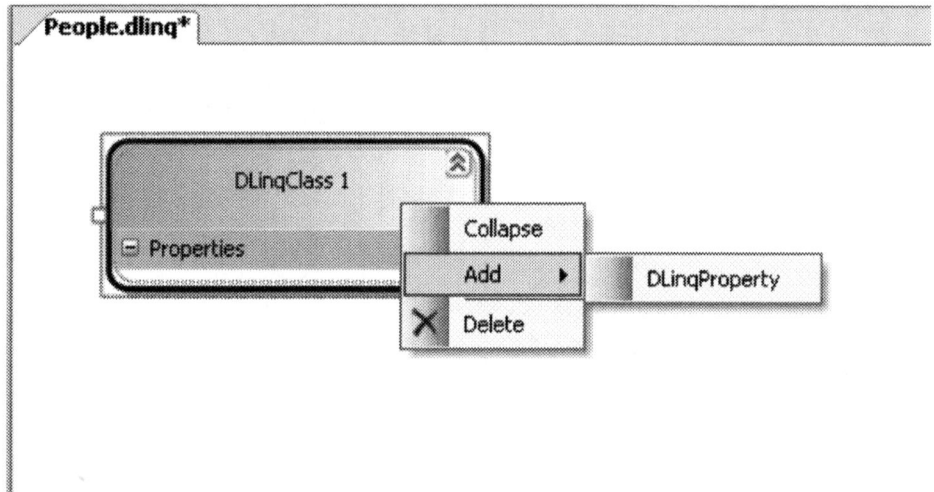

Figure 2-17. After adding a new DLinq class we can add new properties or delete the class itself.

6. Specify properties in the Properties window (see Figure 2-18). You should be accustomed to the property names because they are the same as column attributes.

Figure 2-18. The Properties window shows the DLinqProperty item properties.

7. Because DLinq Designer supports drag-and-drop from Server Explorer, we are not going to create each class manually from the database. If you can't see Server Explorer, select View ➤ Server Explorer. From Server Explorer select the Connect to Database button, as shown in Figure 2-19.

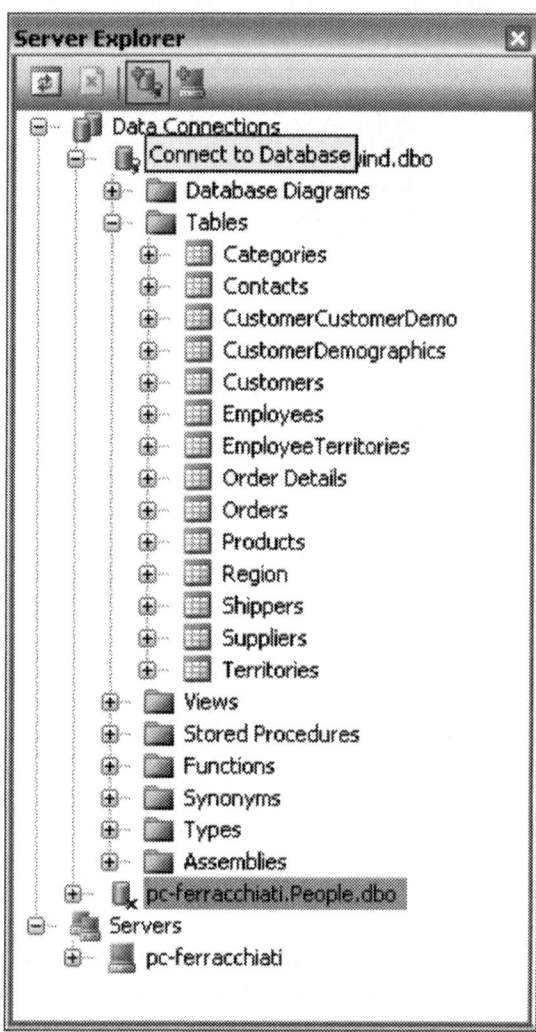

Figure 2-19. Connecting to a database from Server Explorer

8. From the Add Connection dialog box (shown in Figure 2-20) you specify every parameter—server name, database, and so on—to connect to a database. Select the database server where the People database has been stored.

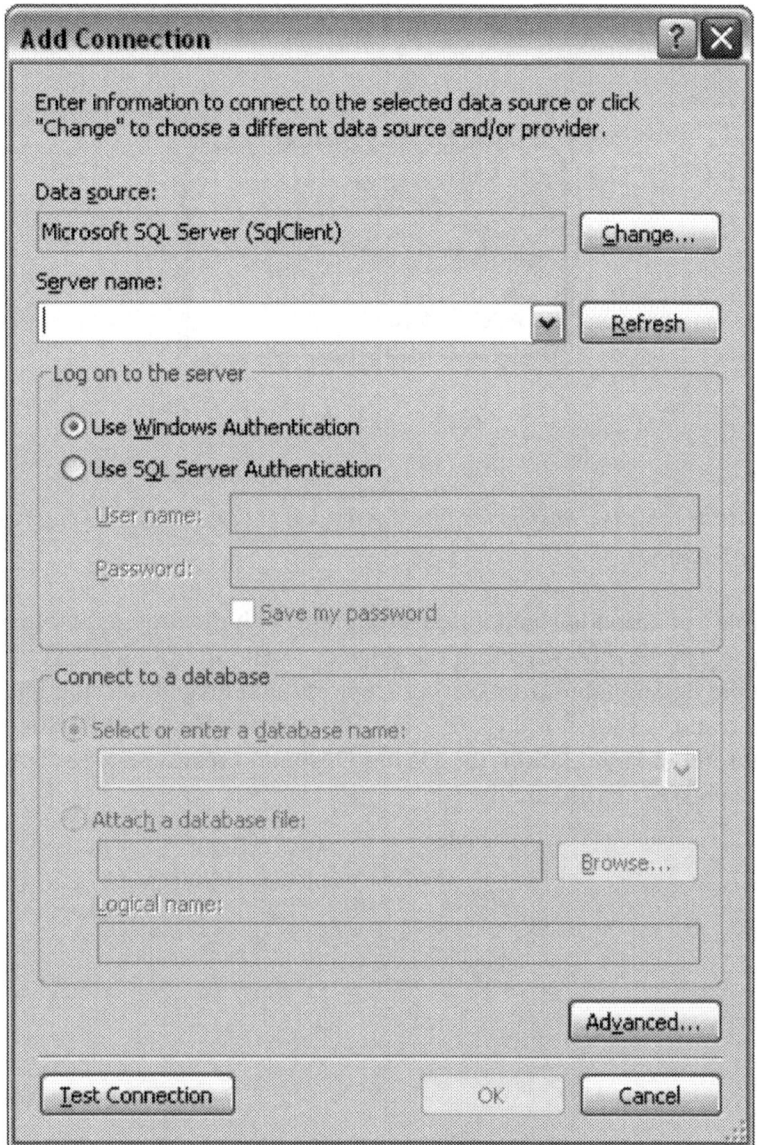

Figure 2-20. Add a connection to a database to manage it from Visual Studio.

9. Choose a table from Server Explorer and drag it into the DLinq Designer tool. For example, using the People database, drag the Role table and drop it into the designer. Visual Studio will present the diagram in Figure 2-21.

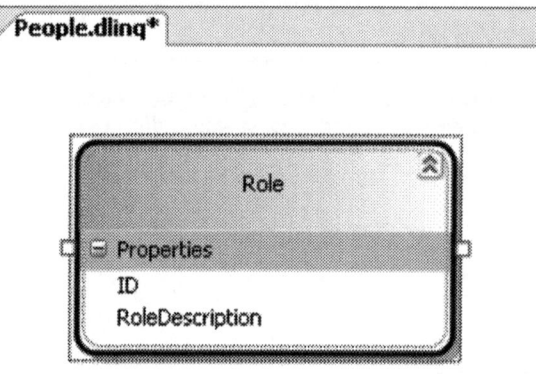

Figure 2-21. The Role table is transformed into the Region entity class after you drag and drop the table from Server Explorer.

10. This simple operation has generated a diagram with the dragged table and some code (which you can view by selecting the related ,vb file in Solution Explorer). Now you can drag the Person table from Server Explorer and drop it into the DLinq Designer. The final result is shown in Figure 2-22. Because the Role and Person tables have defined a foreign key relation, the DLinq Designer creates an association between the two entity classes automatically.

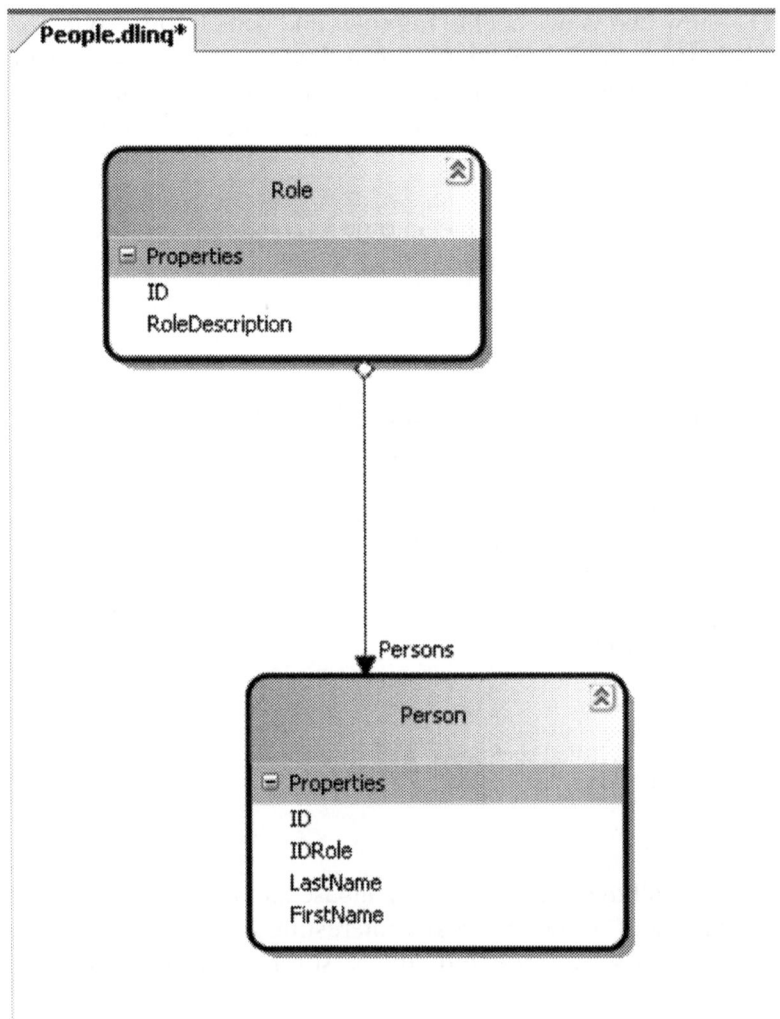

Figure 2-22. The association between the Role and Person tables

---

Caution ➤ A bug has been found in the code generated by the DLinq Designer tool. The association between entity classes is correct, but when the code specifies the delegates to call when a related object is attached or detached, it provides the same delegate. The EntitySet class constructor uses two Notification objects that pass the same Attach argument. You have to change it manually to pass the Detach delegate name as the second argument.

---

11. We want to show two views containing roles and person rows. When we select a row from the Role view, the Person view is refreshed to show related person rows. To accomplish this we can add two DataGridView controls to the main form—one called dgRole that will contain role rows, and the other called dgPerson to contain related person rows.

12. In the Form1 class we have to define an object from the PeopleDataContext class generated by the tool to query the database within the source code:

```
Public Class Form1
    Private db As PeopleDataContext
```

13. Now we have to add the Load event handler in the code, and specify the following code:

```
Private Sub Form1_Load(ByVal sender As System.Object, _
ByVal e As System.EventArgs) Handles MyBase.Load
    db = New PeopleDataContext

    Dim tableRoles = db.Roles
    Dim query = From r In tableRoles _
        Select r

    dgRole.DataSource = query.ToList()
    dgPerson.DataSource = dgRole.DataSource
    dgPerson.DataMember = "Persons"

End Sub
```

The query retrieves all the roles from the database and uses the ToList method to fill the dgRole data grid. The rest of the code is really interesting because it uses the association between the two entity classes to show only the person-related rows in the data grid. It uses just two simple lines of code!

14. Press CTRL + F5 to build and execute the code. Selecting the role rows shows that the dgPerson grid displays related rows (see Figure 2-23).

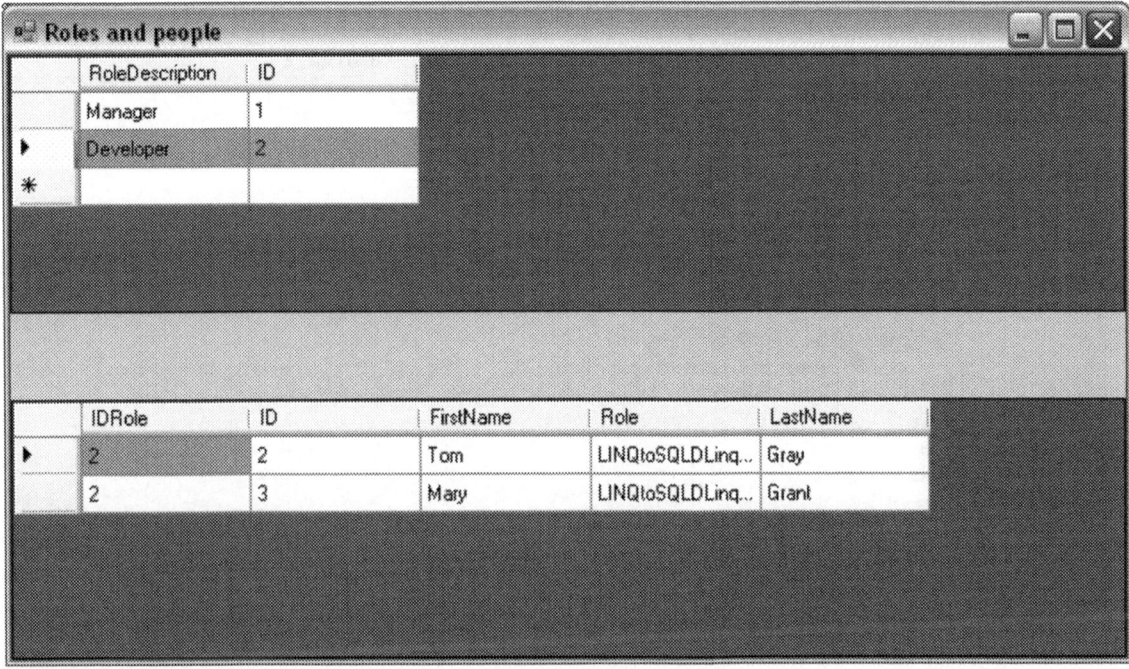

Figure 2-23. The Windows form application in execution

Debugging LINQ Applications

A new tool has been added to the Visual Studio debugger: the SQL Server Query Visualizer. This tool is really useful because it allows us to check the query syntax built by LINQ before it's sent to the database. Moreover, it allows us to execute the query from the debugger to discover if the result is what we expect. We can also modify the query.

    To use the visualizer we have to put a breakpoint just before the LINQ query definition and press the little magnifying-glass icon that appears when we mouse over the query variable (see Figure 2-24).

```
Module1.vb  People.vb
Module1                                                   Listing2_2
    Sub Listing2_2()
        Dim people = New PeopleDataContext()
        Dim tablePeople = people.People
        Dim tableSalaries = people.Salaries

        Dim query = From p In tablePeople, s In tableSalaries
            Where ⊞ query  {System.Data.DLinq.DataQuery(Of LINQToSQL.Module1._Anonymous_Listing2_2_4E_13)}
            Select New {p.LastName, p.FirstName, s.Year, s.SalaryYear}

        For Each Dim record In query
            Console.WriteLine("Name: {0}, {1} - Year: {2}", record.LastName, record.Fi
            Console.WriteLine("Salary: {0}", record.SalaryYear)
        Next
    End Sub
#End Region
```

Figure 2-24. Pressing the magnifying-glass icon to use the SQL Server Query Visualizer

After you press the magnifying-glass icon the Query Visualizer tool will appear within the debugger (see Figure 2-25).

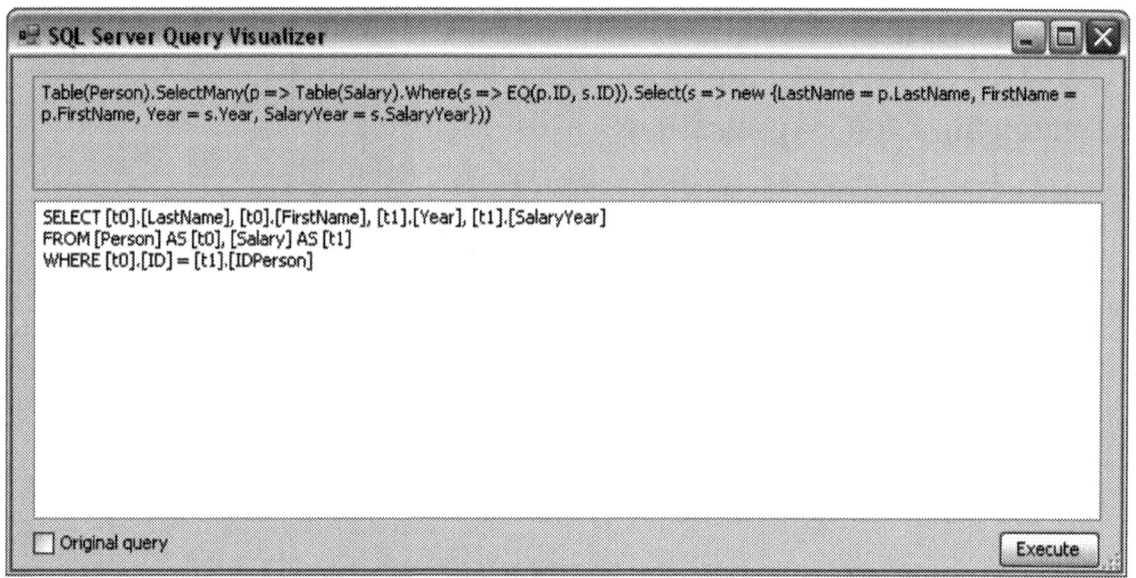

Figure 2-25. The SQL Server Query Visualizer in action

The window is divided in two sections: The upper section is a read-only text area where the LINQ query is displayed after the compiler has transformed it using lambda expressions and methods. The lower section is a writable text area containing the SQL to be executed against the database. You can execute the SQL by clicking the Execute button (see Figure 2-26).

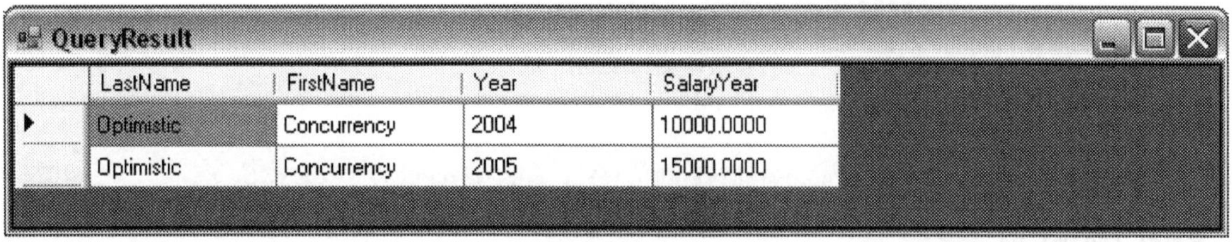

Figure 2-26. Pressing the Execute button provided by the SQL Server Query Visualizer executes the query, showing the result in the QueryResult window while the application is waiting on a breakpoint.

Placing the breakpoint just after the query variable definition illustrates that LINQ to SQL uses deferred query execution. Remember that query execution starts only after the query is iterated through a For Each statement or when a caching method such as ToList() is used. The debugger allows us to discover an additional aspect during query execution. Consider the code snippet in Listing 2-26.

Listing 2-26. Iterating Through Role and Person Rows

```
Dim people As New PeopleDataContext()
people.Log = Console.Out

Dim query = From r In people.Roles _
    Select r

For Each Dim role In query
    For Each Dim person In role.People
        Console.WriteLine("Person: {0} {1}", person.FirstName, _
            person.LastName)
    Next
Next
```

The code uses the association declared in Role and Person entity classes to iterate through role rows and, with an inner For Each statement, to print the persons that have each role.

If you put a breakpoint on the query variable within the For Each statement and press F5 to start the debugger, you'll see that no query has been sent to the database. Press F10 to go a step further; the first query will be printed in the console application (see Figure 2-27).

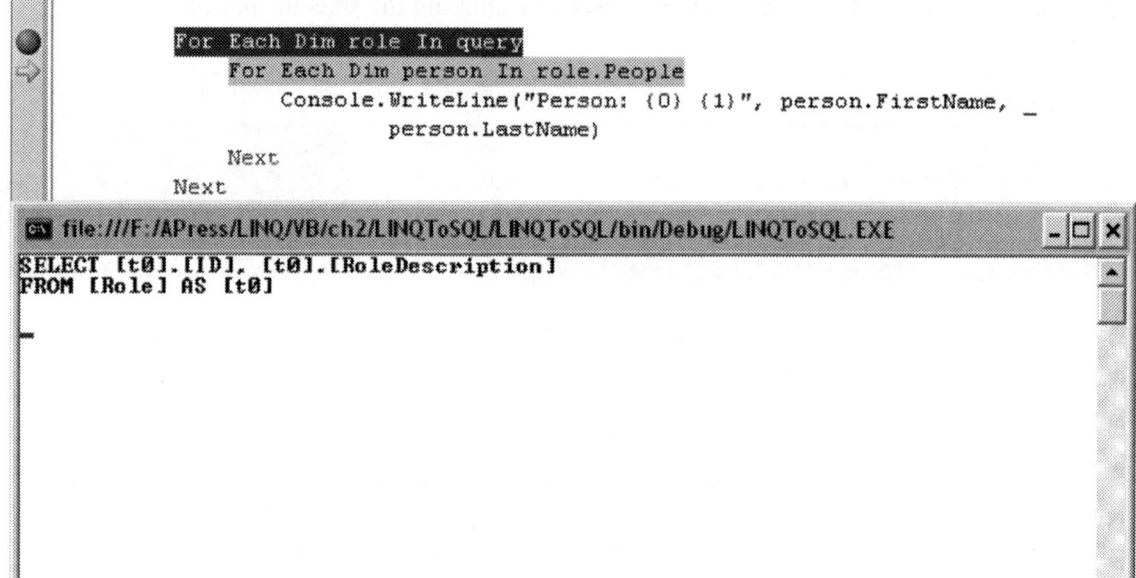

Figure 2-27. The first query is sent to the database just after the query variable is iterated.

Continue pressing F10 to see that a SELECT statement is sent to the database to select person rows each time a new role is processed (see Figure 2-28).

Figure 2-28. Each time a new role row is processed a new SELECT statement is sent to the database to retrieve related person rows.

LINQ to DataSet

In the previous section, you saw how LINQ to SQL supports ADO.NET transactions. This is not the only integration between the "old" ADO.NET library and the "new" LINQ to SQL. In fact, LINQ to SQL can use ADO.NET DataSets with LINQ to DataSet.

With some limitations, LINQ to DataSet allows developers to use DataSets as normal data sources using the usual LINQ query syntax.

Listing 2-27 shows a simple example that uses a LINQ query to fill a typed dataset.

Listing 2-27. Filling a Typed Dataset with the LoadSequence Method

```
Dim ds As New dsPeople()
Dim people As New PeopleDataContext()

Dim q = From r In people.Roles _
    Select r
```

```
ds.Role.LoadSequence(q)
```

Listing2_28(ds)

dsPeople is a typed DataSet added to the Visual Studio project. When you use Visual Studio to create your DataSet objects you can use the DataSet Designer tool, which makes it possible to drag and drop tables from Server Explorer (the same way as when using DLinq Designer). In the dsPeople data set I added the Role table. This operation has automatically created a typed DataSet that contains the Role table together with some other methods and objects.

By using the LoadSequence method provided by the DataTable class we can iterate through LINQ query results and populate the DataTable object. This method is useful to fill an existing DataTable object with rows retrieved by a LINQ query.

But, wait a minute! The LoadSequence method is not a DataTable method in ADO.NET 1.x and 2.0. How is it possible to use it? The answer is the System.Data.Extensions.dll assembly.

Using the method extensions seen in Chapter 1 it's possible to extend a class by providing new methods without releasing a new version of the assembly. The new System.Data.Extensions.dll contains the extension methods necessary to integrate LINQ with ADO.NET.

Note ➤ In existing ADO.NET applications DataSet objects are filled with DataAdapter objects or with other techniques. LINQ to DataSet is completely indifferent about how you fill a DataSet.

In Listing 2-28 we use the filled dsPeople DataSet just like any data source, and a LINQ query to retrieve a role.

Listing 2-28. A Typed DataSet Is Queryable Just Like Any Other Data Source.

```
Sub Listing2_28(ByVal ds As dsPeople)
  Dim query = From r In ds.Role _
      Where r.ID = 1 _
      Select r

  For Each Dim row In query
      Console.WriteLine("Role: {0} {1}", row.ID, row.RoleDescription)
  Next
End Sub
```

The Role property contained in the ds DataSet is iterated by using the Rows collection to look for the row whose identifier is equal to 1.

LINQ to DataSet adds support for untyped DataSets as well. In this case the code is a bit more complex to write because LINQ has to acquire more information from the query. Listing 2-29 shows how an untyped data set can be filled using a LINQ query.

Listing 2-29. Filling an Untyped Data Set Using a LINQ Query and the ToDataTable Method

```
Dim people As New PeopleDataContext()

Dim q = From p In people.People _
    Select p

Dim ds As New DataSet("People")
ds.Tables.Add(q.ToDataTable())

Listing2_30(ds)
```

The code selects each row contained in the Person table and adds a new DataTable into the data-set object. The ToDataTable extended method iterates through the results of the query, creating a new DataTable object filled with DataColumn objects and values.

Querying an untyped data set is a bit more complex because we have to use the Field(Of T) class to specify the column's data type; see Listing 2-30.

Listing 2-30. The Code Using an Untyped Data Set Is More Complex and Less Readable.

```
Sub Listing2_30(ByVal ds As DataSet)
    Dim dtPerson As DataTable = ds.Tables(0)

    Dim person = dtPerson.ToQueryable()

    Dim query = From p In person _
        Where p.Field(Of String)("LastName") = "Grant" _
        Select p

    For Each Dim row In query
        Console.WriteLine("Person: {0} {1}", _
                            row.Field(Of String)("FirstName"), _
                            row.Field(Of String)("LastName"))

    Next

End Sub
```

First of all, the DataTable class doesn't provide an implementation of the IEnumerable and IQueryable interfaces, so the dtPerson object cannot be used in the LINQ query directly. We have to use the ToQueryable extended method, which generates a Sequence composed of DataTable rows.

Note ➤ When using the LoadSequence method we don't need to call the ToQueryable method for the DataTable object—it is called internally.

Second, we need to use the Field(Of T) generic method to specify the data type of the DataTable column we are going to manage. This is necessary because when using the classic syntax to access a DataTable row (e.g. p("LastName")) we should cast the return type and also use the IsNull method of the DataRow class to check if the data is null. The Field(Of T) generic method does all this automatically, plus checks null values when the column accepts nulls (e.g., using Field(Of Nullable(Of String))).

As stated previously, LINQ to DataSet has some limitations that should be removed eventually. For example, the ToDataTable method doesn't understand relationships and cannot produce multiple data tables. Moreover, there is no way to use LINQ to DataSet to update database rows after they are retrieved by a LINQ query into a data set object.

Summary

In this chapter you saw how to create entity classes and how, thanks to new attributes and their properties, you can easily map those classes to database tables. Then you analyzed DataContext functionality for interfacing with databases. You also saw how defining associations between entity classes simulates relationships between tables.

You then looked at advanced features, such as optimistic concurrency, stored procedures, and user-defined functions.

Finally, you used the Visual Studio DLinq Designer tool to create entity classes, and you used its improved debugger. The chapter concluded by analyzing LINQ integration with ADO.NET, specifically with DataSets.

In the next chapter we'll use LINQ to manage XML data.

CHAPTER 3

LINQ to XML

In this chapter we'll analyze LINQ to XML in detail. We'll start by viewing XML documents as data sources and then we'll use LINQ queries to retrieve XML data. Finally we'll look at how to use LINQ to XML to produce XML documents.

Introduction

Language-Integrated Query lets you focus on what you have to do and not on how to do it. With this in mind, XML becomes just another data source for LINQ.

From a developer perspective, XML is not an easy thing to manage because the World Wide Web Consortium's document object model (DOM) is not a simple library to use. The DOM framework often requires you to write a lot of code to produce even a little XML output. Moreover, if you need to search for a particular item within an XML document you have to use DOM features, such as XPath, based on query syntax that is not intuitive. XPath uses a searching model that is not similar to other query languages, such as SQL, and you have to spend time to learn it.

Eliminating such complexity is the main motive behind LINQ to XML. .NET offers its own library to manage XML, but LINQ to XML goes a big step further; it integrates the LINQ standard query operators with XML documents. In addition, LINQ to XML offers classes for easily creating XML.

Querying XML

Since LINQ to XML supports the LINQ standard query operators, an XML document can be loaded in memory and then queried with the usual LINQ query syntax.

Let's start by analyzing a simple query using a couple of important LINQ to XML classes. Listing 3-1 is the XML representation of our People database.

Listing 3-1. The XML Representation of the People Database

```
<?xml version="1.0" encoding="utf-8" ?>
<people>
        <!--Person section-->
```

```xml
<person>
        <id>1</id>
        <firstname>Carl</firstname>
        <lastname>Lewis</lastname>
        <idrole>1</idrole>
</person>
<person>
        <id>2</id>
        <firstname>Tom</firstname>
        <lastname>Gray</lastname>
        <idrole>2</idrole>
</person>
<person>
        <id>3</id>
        <firstname>Mary</firstname>
        <lastname>Grant</lastname>
        <idrole>2</idrole>
</person>
<person>
        <id>4</id>
        <firstname>Fabio Claudio</firstname>
        <lastname>Ferracchiati</lastname>
        <idrole>1</idrole>
</person>
<!--Role section-->
<role>
        <id>1</id>
        <roledescription>Manager</roledescription>
</role>
<role>
        <id>2</id>
        <roledescription>Developer</roledescription>
</role>
<!--Salary section-->
<salary>
        <idperson id="1" year="2004" salaryyear="10000,0000" />
        <idperson id="1" year="2005" salaryyear="15000,0000" />
</salary>
</people>
```

In Listing 3-1 the XDocument class provides the Elements method that returns items from the XElement class. The XElement class represents the core of the entire LINQ to XML library. An XElement object is the representation of an element within an XML document.

Each node, as well as each leaf, in the XML document is an element. As you can see from the code in Listing 3-2, to obtain an element's value you have to use the Elements method repeatedly. When observing the XML structure you can see that the people element is the root and the person element appears four times to represent four rows in the people data source. Using the Elements method provided by the XElement class you can retrieve a collection of elements and iterate through them. So, by appending the Elements("person") method call to the Elements("people") method call you can retrieve all four person elements in the XML document.

The Where condition filters the person elements to retrieve the one whose identifier is equal to 1.

Listing 3-2. Retrieving a Person's Record from an XML Document

```
Dim xml As XDocument = XDocument.Load("..\..\People.xml")

Dim query = From p In xml.Elements("people").Elements("person") _
    Where p.Element("id").Value = 1 _
    Select p

For Each Dim record In query
    Console.WriteLine("Person: {0} {1}", _
        record.Element("firstname").Value, _
        record.Element("lastname").Value)
Next
```

Note ➡ With respect to the C# compiler, the VB compiler is not able to cast the Where condition parameter unless you manually add the Value property to the Element item.

Finally, the For Each statement iterates through the elements and prints the name of each person. You use the Value property to retrieve an element's value.

The XDocument class is very similar to the XElement class (it contains the same methods, properties, etc.) but it represents the root element of an XML document. In our example, the XDocument object represents the people element. Its Load method will load the XML document into memory, allowing us to use the XDocument object for queries.

If you don't care about the root element and just want to go straight to a particular element, you can use the Load method of the XElement class. In Listing 3-3 you can see the same query applied to our XML data source but using less code.

Listing 3-3. Retrieving Person Data by Using Less Code

```
Dim xml As XElement = XElement.Load("..\..\People.xml")

Dim query = From p In xml.Elements("person") _
    Where p.Element("id").value = 1 _
    Select p

For Each Dim record In query
    Console.WriteLine("Person: {0} {1}", _
                record.Element("firstname"), _
                record.Element("lastname"))
Next
```

You can search directly for person records without calling the Elements method for the root element. Moreover, if you omit the Value property (used in Listing 3-2), you can call the ToString method, which returns the full element with its start and end tags (see Figure 3-1).

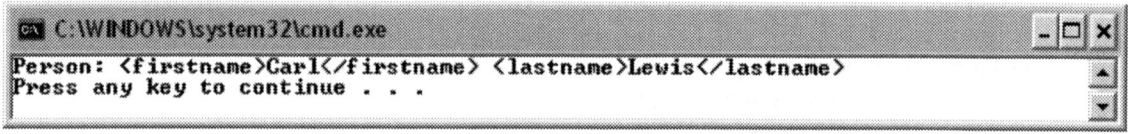

Figure 3-1. When omitting the Value property, the output will be the full element.

Note ➡ Casting an Element to a string is equivalent to using its Value property.

Searching for Attribute Values

The following code shows salary information stored in idperson attributes:

```
<salary>
        <idperson year="2004" salaryyear="10000,0000">1</idperson>
        <idperson year="2005" salaryyear="15000,0000">1</idperson>
</salary>
```

Obviously, LINQ to XML provides a way to query elements by their attributes. (See Listing 3-4.)

Listing 3-4. Querying by Attribute Values

```
Dim xml As XElement = XElement.Load("..\..\People.xml")

Dim query = From s In xml.Elements("salary").Elements("idperson") _
    Where s.Attribute("year").Value = 2004 _
    Select s

For Each Dim record In query
    Console.WriteLine("Amount: {0}", record.Attribute("salaryyear"))
Next
```

The XAttribute class represents the attributes of an element within an XML document. The Attribute method returns the value of the attribute whose name is specified as its argument.

The Descendants and Ancestors Methods

When elements are deeply nested, you can use the Descendants method to quickly navigate to the desired element. Listing 3-5 shows how to navigate down into nested elements using this quicker way.

Listing 3-5. Using the Descendants Method to Navigate Down an XML Tree

```
Dim xml As XElement = XElement.Load("..\..\People.xml")

Dim query = From p In xml.Descendants("person"), s In xml.Descendants("idperson") _
    Where p.Element("id").Value = s.Attribute("id").Value _
    Select New {FirstName := p.Element("firstname").Value, _
                LastName := p.Element("lastname").Value, _
                Amount := s.Attribute("salaryyear").Value}

For Each Dim record In query
    Console.WriteLine("Person: {0} {1}, Salary {2}", record.FirstName, _
                        record.LastName, _
                        record.Amount)
Next
```

The code in Listing 3-5 joins two sections within the XML data source: person and salary. As you can see, the query syntax is the same as that used for in-memory objects and database tables and views.

Conversely, the Ancestors method goes up through an XML tree until it reaches the root element. In Listing 3-6, both methods are used to navigate the XML document.

Listing 3-6. Using the Ancestors and Descendents Methods to Navigate in the XML Document Tree

```
Dim xml As XElement = XElement.Load("..\..\People.xml")

Dim record = xml.Descendants("firstname").First()
For Each Dim tag In record.Ancestors()
    Console.WriteLine(tag.Name)
Next
```

First the Descendants method returns a collection of firstname elements; however, if we use the First standard operator, just the first element will be retrieved. The cursor in the XML tree now points to the first firstname element, containing the Carl value, so if we use the Ancestors method to rise to the top of the document, the collection of XElement's items will contain two tags: person and people.

Note ➡ The Descendants and Ancestors methods do not include the current node. For example, if you start from the root node you'll retrieve all the elements except the root. You can use the SelfAndDescendants and SelfAndAncestors methods to include the current node.

Querying XML for Content Type

We can use LINQ to XML to query not only for values, but also for types. For instance, our sample XML data source contains three comments. We can search for all the comments as in Listing 3-7.

Listing 3-7. Retrieving All the Comments in an XML Document

```
Dim xml As XElement = XElement.Load("..\..\People.xml")

Dim record As IEnumerable(Of XComment) = xml.Nodes().OfType(Of XComment)()
For Each comment As XComment In record
    Console.WriteLine(comment)
Next
```

The XComment class represents XML comments. Note that we used the Nodes method instead of the Elements method. Examine Figure 3-2 carefully to better understand the hierarchy between LINQ to XML classes.

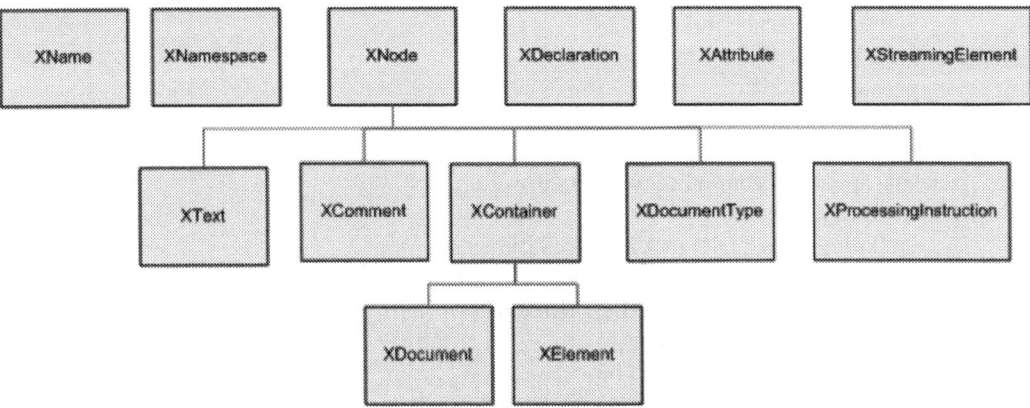

Figure 3-2. The LINQ to XML class hierarchy

The XElement class is not directly linked to the XComment class, so if we want to retrieve comments we have to use the XNode class. For this reason,, by using the Nodes method of XElement we can obtain a collection of Node objects. Using the OfType standard operator we can filter the objects for the specified type—in Listing 3-7, XComment.

Querying an XML Document That Uses Schemas

XML elements are often associated with specific namespaces, and their names are prefixed with a namespace identifier. For example, Microsoft Office 2003 adds XML support for applications such as Microsoft Word, Microsoft Excel, and so on. If you save a simple Word file in XML format, you get an XML document similar to the snippet in Listing 3-8.

Listing 3-8. A Microsoft Word Document Saved Using the XML Format

```
<?xml version="1.0" encoding="UTF-8" standalone="yes"?>
<?mso-application progid="Word.Document"?>
<w:wordDocument
xmlns:w="http://schemas.microsoft.com/office/word/2003/wordml"
            xmlns:v="urn:schemas-microsoft-com:vml"
            xmlns:w10="urn:schemas-microsoft-com:office:word"
            xmlns:sl="http://schemas.microsoft.com/schemaLibrary/2003/core"
            xmlns:aml="http://schemas.microsoft.com/aml/2001/core"
```

```
                    xmlns:wx="http://schemas.microsoft.com/office/word/2003/auxHint"
                    xmlns:o="urn:schemas-microsoft-com:office:office"
                    xmlns:dt="uuid:C2F41010-65B3-11d1-A29F-00AA00C14882"
                    xmlns:wsp="http://schemas.microsoft.com/office/word/2003/wordml/sp2"
                    w:macrosPresent="no"
                    w:embeddedObjPresent="no"
                    w:ocxPresent="no"
                    xml:space="preserve">
<w:ignoreElements
w:val="http://schemas.microsoft.com/office/word/2003/wordml/sp2"/>
        <o:DocumentProperties>
                <o:Title>Hello LINQ to XML</o:Title>
                <o:Author>Fabio Claudio Ferracchiati</o:Author>
                <o:LastAuthor>Fabio Claudio Ferracchiati</o:LastAuthor>
                <o:Revision>1</o:Revision>
                <o:TotalTime>1</o:TotalTime>
                <o:Created>2006-08-20T07:54:00Z</o:Created>
                <o:LastSaved>2006-08-20T07:55:00Z</o:LastSaved>
                <o:Pages>1</o:Pages>
                <o:Words>1</o:Words>
                <o:Characters>12</o:Characters>
                <o:Company>APress</o:Company>
                <o:Lines>1</o:Lines>
                <o:Paragraphs>1</o:Paragraphs>
                <o:CharactersWithSpaces>12</o:CharactersWithSpaces>
                <o:Version>11.8026</o:Version>
        </o:DocumentProperties>
        <w:fonts>
                <w:defaultFonts
w:ascii="Times New Roman"
                                w:fareast="Times New Roman"
                                w:h-ansi="Times New Roman"
                                w:cs="Times New Roman"/>
        </w:fonts>
...
...
...

</w:wordDocument>
```

To query for the Word file's author, we have to search for the <o:Author> tag. The o: prefix identifies the XML namespace defined as

```
            xmlns:o="urn:schemas-microsoft-com:office:office"
```

We have to add this information to our LINQ to XML code as shown in Listing 3-9.

Listing 3-9. Querying an XML Document That Uses Namespaces

```
Dim xml As XElement = XElement.Load("..\..\Hello_XLINQ.xml")
Dim o As XNamespace = "urn:schemas-microsoft-com:office:office"

Dim query = From w In xml.Descendants(o + "Author") _
    Select w

For Each Dim record In query
    Console.WriteLine("Author: {0}", record.Value)
Next
```

The XNamespace class represents and XML namespace. If we concatenate the o object with "Author", the Descendants method will go through the XML document until it reaches the Author tag for the namespace represented by the o object.

You can search for a particular attribute in a similar way. In Listing 3-10 the code searches for the default font style used in the Word document.

Listing 3-10. Retrieving the Attribute's Value Prefixed with the Namespace Shortcut

```
Dim xml As XElement = XElement.Load("..\..\Hello_XLINQ.xml")
Dim w As XNamespace = "http://schemas.microsoft.com/office/word/2003/wordml"

Dim defaultFonts As XElement = xml.Descendants(w + "defaultFonts").First()
Console.WriteLine("Default Fonts: {0}", _
    defaultFonts.Attribute(w + "ascii").Value)
```

After the Descendants method reached the first w:DefaultFonts element, we used the XElement object's Attribute method to retrieve the w:ascii attribute. Note that the namespace must be concatenated to the attribute name in the same way as for the parent element.

The ElementsBeforeThis and ElementsAfterThis Methods

It's often necessary to retrieve child elements starting from the current node. This is easy to do by using the ElementsBeforeThis and ElementsAfterThis methods, which retrieve a collection of sibling XElement items that occur before the current element and after the current element, respectively. Listing 3-11 shows both methods in action.

Listing 3-11. Using the ElementsBeforeThis and ElementsAfterThis Methods

```
Dim xml As XElement = XElement.Load("..\..\People.xml")

Dim firstName As XElement = xml.Descendants("firstname").First()

Console.WriteLine("Before <firstname>")
For Each Dim tag In firstName.ElementsBeforeThis()
    Console.WriteLine(tag.Name)
Next

Console.WriteLine("")
Console.WriteLine("After <firstname>")
For Each Dim tag In firstName.ElementsAfterThis()
    Console.WriteLine(tag.Name)
Next
```

After we've positioned the cursor over the first firstname element, calling the two methods will produce the output shown in Figure 3-3.

Figure 3-3. The output shows the XML tags before and after the current XML tag.

Note ➡ If you want to retrieve other XML information, such as comments, you have to use the Node versions of ElementsBeforeThis and ElementsAfterThis, NodesBeforeThis and NodesAfterThis.

Miscellaneous Functionalities

The XElement class provides other useful properties to easily obtain access to XML-document information. In this section we will look at them individually.

Parent

This property allows us to retrieve the parent element of the current node, as Listing 3-12 shows.

Listing 3-12. Using the Parent Property to Retrieve the Parent Node of the firstname Element

```
Dim xml As XElement = XElement.Load("..\..\People.xml")

Dim firstName As XElement = xml.Descendants("firstname").First()

Console.WriteLine(firstName.Parent)
```

The parent node of firstname is person, so the output of this code snippet will be the full person element (see Figure 3-4).

```
<person>
  <id>1</id>
  <firstname>Carl</firstname>
  <lastname>Lewis</lastname>
  <idrole>1</idrole>
</person>
Press any key to continue . . .
```

Figure 3-4. The output of the code snippet in Listing 3-12

HasElements and HasAttributes

These properties check if the current element has child elements or attributes. (See Listing 3-13.)

Listing 3-13. Using HasElements and HasAttributes to Check If the Current Node Has Child Elements and Attributes, Respectively

```
Dim xml As XElement = XElement.Load("..\..\People.xml")

Dim firstName As XElement = xml.Descendants("firstname").First()

Console.WriteLine("FirstName tag has attributes: {0}", _
    firstName.HasAttributes)
Console.WriteLine("FirstName tag has child elements: {0}", _
    firstName.HasElements)
Console.WriteLine("FirstName tag's parent has attributes: {0}", _
```

```
        firstName.Parent.HasAttributes)
    Console.WriteLine("FirstName tag's parent has child elements: {0}", _
        firstName.Parent.HasElements)
```

After the cursor reaches the first firstname element by using the Descendants method, the HasAttributes and HasElements properties check if both the firstname element and its parent have attributes and child elements. Figure 3-5 shows the output of this code snippet.

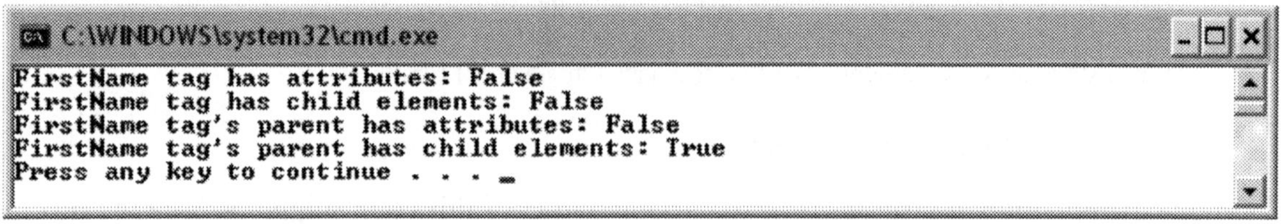

Figure 3-5. The HasElements and HasAttributes properties in action

IsEmpty

This property checks if the current element contains a value or whether it is empty. (See Listing 3-14.)

Listing 3-14. Using the IsEmpty Property to Check If Some Elements Are Empty

```
    Dim xml As XElement = XElement.Load("..\..\People.xml")

    Dim firstName As XElement = xml.Descendants("firstname").First()

    Console.WriteLine("Is FirstName tag empty? {0}", Iif(firstName.IsEmpty, "Yes", "No"))

    Dim idPerson As XElement = xml.Descendants("idperson").First()

    Console.WriteLine("Is idperson tag empty? {0}", Iif(idPerson.IsEmpty, "Yes", "No"))
```

Figure 3-6 shows the output of this code snippet. If you look at the XML data source (Listing 3-1) you'll see that the firstname element is not empty because it contains the Carl value. You'll also see that the idperson tag is empty (and has only attributes).

Figure 3-6. The output of the code snippet using IsEmpty

Declaration

Using this property we can retrieve information about the XML document declaration. In Listing 3-15 we load the XML document using the XDocument class because it fills the LINQ to XML classes with all the possible information, such as the XML declaration, namespaces, and so on. We also use the Declaration property to retrieve Encoding, Version, and Standalone information from the XML document declaration.

Listing 3-15. Using the Declaration Property

```
Dim xml As XDocument = XDocument.Load("..\..\Hello_XLINQ.xml")

Console.WriteLine("Encoding: {0}", xml.Declaration.Encoding)
Console.WriteLine("Version: {0}", xml.Declaration.Version)
Console.WriteLine("Standalone: {0}", xml.Declaration.Standalone)
```

Figure 3-7 shows the output of Listing 3-15.

Figure 3-7. The output of the code snippet using the Declaration property

Creating and Modifying XML Documents

LINQ to XML doesn't only provide for queries; it also provides for creating and modifying XML documents. Thanks to a feature called *functional construction*, you can create XML documents in an easier way than with the W3C DOM library.

We'll use functional construction to create an XML document from scratch, and then use other LINQ to XML features to manage it.

Finally, we'll look at a couple of examples that integrate LINQ to XML with LINQ to SQL to generate XML output from a database query.

Creating an XML Document from Scratch

If you are accustomed to using the W3C DOM library or the .NET Framework implementation of it, you'll find LINQ to XML very easy and more intuitive to use. The very simple code snippet that follows creates a new person element, followed by its elements:

```
Dim xml As New XElement("people", _
        New XElement("person", _
           New XElement("id", 1), _
           New XElement("firstname", "Carl"), _
           New XElement("lastname", "Lewis"), _
           New XElement("idrole", 2)))
```

The functional construction model allows us to use the LINQ to XML classes in a "linked" way. You can create objects with a hierarchical structure that it is similar to the one used in an XML document. Moreover, it is a top-down approach to XML document creation that is more intuitive than the bottom-up approach of the W3C libraries. So the first element to create is the root, people:

```
Dim xml As New XElement("people", _
```

To its constructor we can pass another XElement object (person) that will become the child element of people:

```
Dim xml As New XElement("people", _
        New XElement("person", _
```

We pass other XElement objects to the person constructor to define its children:

```
        New XElement("person", _
           New XElement("id", 1), _
           New XElement("firstname", "Carl"), _
           New XElement("lastname", "Lewis"), _
           New XElement("idrole", 2)))
```

The XML document will look like this:

```
<people>
 <person>
  <id>1</id>
```

```
      <firstname>Carl</firstname>
      <lastname>Lewis</lastname>
      <idrole>2</idrole>
    </person>
</people>
```

Functional construction is based on the XElement class's constructor, which accepts an array of param objects:

```
Public Sub New ( _
      name As XName, _
      ParamArray content As Object() _
)
```

Because this constructor accepts an array of generic object types, we can pass it any kind of information, such as the following:

- An XElement object that will be added as child element

- An XAttribute object that will be used as an attribute for the current element

- A string value that will be used as a value for the current element

- A null value that will be ignored

- An IEnumerable object that will be enumerated and its elements added recursively into the XML document

- A value (variable, constant, property, or method call) to be used as value for the current element

- An XComment object that will be added as child element

- An XProcessingInstruction object that will generate a processing instruction as a child element

Using the XDeclaration Class

You can use an XDocument object to specify the XML declaration, as in Listing 3-16.

Listing 3-16. Using the XDocument Class Constructor to Specify XML Declaration Attributes

```
Dim xml As New XDocument(New XDeclaration("1.0", "UTF-8", "yes"), _
      New XElement("people", _
      New XElement("idperson", _
      New XAttribute("id", 1), _
```

```
            New XAttribute("year", 2004), _
            New XAttribute("salaryyear", "10000,0000"))))

    Dim sw As New System.IO.StringWriter()
    xml.Save(sw)
    Console.WriteLine(sw)
```

Caution ➡ There is a bug in the XDeclaration constructor. Even if you set the encoding value to a value other than UTF-16, UTF-16 will be used.

Listing 3-16 also shows using XAttribute to add attribute values to the current element. Moreover, the Save method, provided by both the XDocument and XElement classes, saves the complete XML document into a StringWriter object (see "Loading and Saving XML" later in this chapter). Figure 3-8 shows the output of Listing 3-16.

```
C:\WINDOWS\system32\cmd.exe
<?xml version="1.0" encoding="utf-16" standalone="yes"?>
<people>
  <idperson id="1" year="2004" salaryyear="10000,0000" />
</people>
Press any key to continue . . .
```

Figure 3-8. Functional construction allows us to easily create part of the People XML document.

Using the XNamespace Class to Create an XML Document

If you need to use XML namespace declarations, use the XNamespace class. Using it to create an XML document is similar to using it to query elements and attributes. We have to use the namespace variable in the XElement class constructor (or in the XAttribute class if we are going to specify an attribute), and add the string that represents the name of the element or the attribute.

Listing 3-17 shows how to produce the first three rows of the Hello_XLINQ.xml Microsoft Word XML file used during previous examples.

Listing 3-17. Reproducing an XML Document Snippet That Has Microsoft Word Format

```
Dim w As XNamespace = "http://schemas.microsoft.com/office/word/2003/wordml"

Dim word As New XDocument(New XDeclaration("1.0", "utf-8", "yes"), _
        New XProcessingInstruction("mso-application", _
          "progid=""Word.Document"""), _
        New XElement(w + "wordDocument", _
        New XAttribute(XNamespace.Xmlns + "w", _
          w.Uri)))

Dim sw As New System.IO.StringWriter()
word.Save(sw)

Console.WriteLine(sw)
```

The bold code shows how to add a namespace and how to add an element and attribute associated with that namespace. The output of this code is as follows:

```
<?xml version="1.0" encoding="UTF-8" standalone="yes"?>
<?mso-application progid="Word.Document"?>
<w:wordDocument xmlns:w="http://schemas.microsoft.com/office/word/2003/wordml" />
```

Transforming XML

A really cool feature of the XElement class constructor is that it can take an IEnumerable(Of XElement) collection as an argument. The constructor will iterate automatically through the collection and create child elements of the current element.

This kind of collection is usually produced by a LINQ query, so we could query an XML document and produce a new XML document with different characteristics. This process is called *XML transformation*, and it's usually done with the W3C's XSL Transformations (XSLT) language.

However, by using functional construction and providing an IEnumerable collection to XElement's constructor we can easily transform an XML document using LINQ to XML.

In Listing 3-18 some information within the People XML document is transformed into an HTML table.

Listing 3-18. Transforming an XML Document into HTML Code

```
Dim xml As XElement = XElement.Load("..\..\People.xml")

Dim html As New XElement("HTML", _
            New XElement("BODY", _
              New XElement("TABLE", _
                New XElement("TH", "ID"), _
                New XElement("TH", "Full Name"), _
                New XElement("TH", "Role"), _
      From p In xml.Descendants("person"), r In xml.Descendants("role") _
      Where p.Element("idrole").Value = r.Element("id").Value _
        Select New XElement("TR", _
                    New XElement("TD", p.Element("id").Value), _
                    New XElement("TD", p.Element("firstname").Value _
                    & " " & p.Element("lastname").Value), _
                    New XElement("TD", r.Element("roledescription").Value)))))

html.Save("C:\People.html")
```

The bold code in Listing 3-18 is the LINQ to XML query used to create the HTML table content. It joins person information in the XML document with role information. Then it selects the values that correspond to the HTML columns declared in the HTML header. The output is then saved into an HTML page using the Save method (see Figure 3-9).

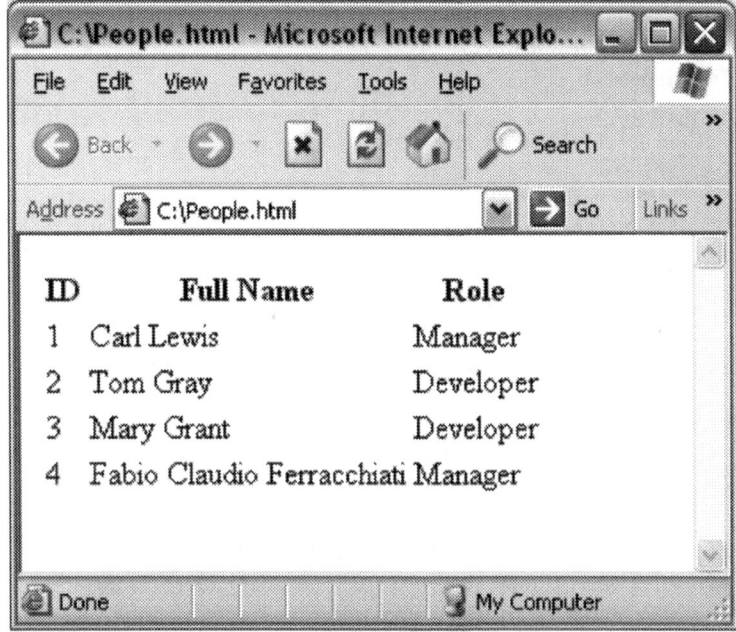

Figure 3-9. The People XML document transformed into HTML

Loading and Saving XML

LINQ to XML provides easy methods to load and saveXML documents. You've already used Load and Save in some of the examples in this chapter. The Load method you've used accepts a string argument that specifies the path where the XML file is located. Similarly, the Save method accepts a string argument in which you specify the path to store the XML document. However, these methods have other interesting overloads that we we'll look at soon.

Also, some other methods deserve mention. For example, the Parse method provided by the XElement class allows developers to build an XML document starting from a string (see Listing 3-19).

Listing 3-19. Building an XML Document from a String

```
Dim doc As String = "<people>" & _
        "<!-- Person section -->" & _
          "<person>" & _
          "<id>1</id>" & _
          "<firstname>Carl</firstname>" & _
```

```
        "<lastname>Lewis</lastname>" & _
        "<idrole>1</idrole>" & _
        "</person>" & _
        "</people>"
Dim xml As XElement = XElement.Parse(doc)
Console.WriteLine(xml)
```

If you use the .NET XmlReader and XmlWriter classes to read and write XML documents, you can pass these objects to the Load and Save methods. Listing 3-20 shows how to use XmlReader and XmlWriter with Load() and Save().

Listing 3-20. Reading an XML Document with XmlReader and Saving It with XmlWriter

```
Dim reader As XmlReader = XmlReader.Create("..\..\People.xml")
Dim xml As XDocument = XDocument.Load(reader)
Console.WriteLine(xml)

Dim idperson As XElement = xml.Descendants("idperson").Last()
idperson.Add(New XElement("idperson", _
        New XAttribute("id", 1), _
        New XAttribute("year", 2006), _
        New XAttribute("salaryyear", "160000,0000")))

Dim sw As New IO.StringWriter()
Dim w As XmlWriter = XmlWriter.Create(sw)
xml.Save(w)
w.Close()
Console.WriteLine(sw.ToString())
```

The static Create method creates an XmlReader object and reads the XML document from the path specified as the argument:

```
Dim reader As XmlReader = XmlReader.Create("..\..\People.xml")
```

Then the XDocument's Load method loads the XmlReader object, building the LINQ to XML document structure:

```
Dim xml As XDocument = XDocument.Load(reader)
```

Similarly, the static Create method creates an XmlWriter object based on a StringWriter object:

```
Dim sw As New IO.StringWriter()
Dim w As XmlWriter = XmlWriter.Create(sw)
```

This is necessary when you want to write the XML output to a string. The Save method provided by the XDocument class (the same as for the XElement class) accepts the XmlWriter object and stores the changes to the XML document in the StringWriter object.

Figure 3-10 shows that a new idperson element has been added to the source XML document.

```
          C:\WINDOWS\system32\cmd.exe
                      <roledescription>Developer</roledescription>
          </role>
          <!-- Salary section -->
          <salary>
                      <idperson id="1" year="2004" salaryyear="10000,0000" />
                      <idperson id="1" year="2005" salaryyear="15000,0000"><idperson i
d="1" year="2006" salaryyear="160000,0000" /></idperson>
          </salary>
</people>

Press any key to continue . . . _
```

Figure 3-10. The salary element has a new idperson child.

Listing 3-20 previewed the code to modify an XML document. In the next section you'll see how to modify XML documents with XElement methods.

Modifying XML

LINQ to XML provides all the methods needed to insert, modify, and delete elements in an existing XML document.

Inserting Elements in an XML Document

In the following code snippet (a duplicate of Listing 3-20) the code that adds a new element to the XML document appears in boldface:

```
Dim reader As XmlReader = XmlReader.Create("..\..\People.xml")
Dim xml As XDocument = XDocument.Load(reader)
Console.WriteLine(xml)

Dim idperson As XElement = xml.Descendants("idperson").Last()
idperson.Add(New XElement("idperson", _
        New XAttribute("id", 1), _
        New XAttribute("year", 2006), _
        New XAttribute("salaryyear", "160000,0000")))
```

```
Dim sw As New IO.StringWriter()
Dim w As XmlWriter = XmlWriter.Create(sw)
xml.Save(w)
w.Close()
Console.WriteLine(sw.ToString())
```

To add an element to a specific position in an XML document, we have to navigate to the desired node using the Element or Descendants methods. Then, using the Add method of XElement, we can add the element in the right place.

Note ➡ If you use the Add method without establishing a specific XML document position, the new element will be added at the end of the document.

We can use the AddFirst method to insert a new element at the beginning of an XML document, just after the root element, as in Listing 3-21.

Listing 3-21. Using AddFirst to Insert a New Element at the Beginning of an XML Document

```
Dim xml As XElement = XElement.Load("..\..\People.xml")

xml.AddFirst(New XElement("person", _
        New XElement("id", 5), _
        New XElement("firstname", "Tom"), _
        New XElement("lastname", "Cruise"), _
        New XElement("idrole", 1)))

Console.WriteLine(xml)
```

Figure 3-11 shows the output for Listing 3-21.

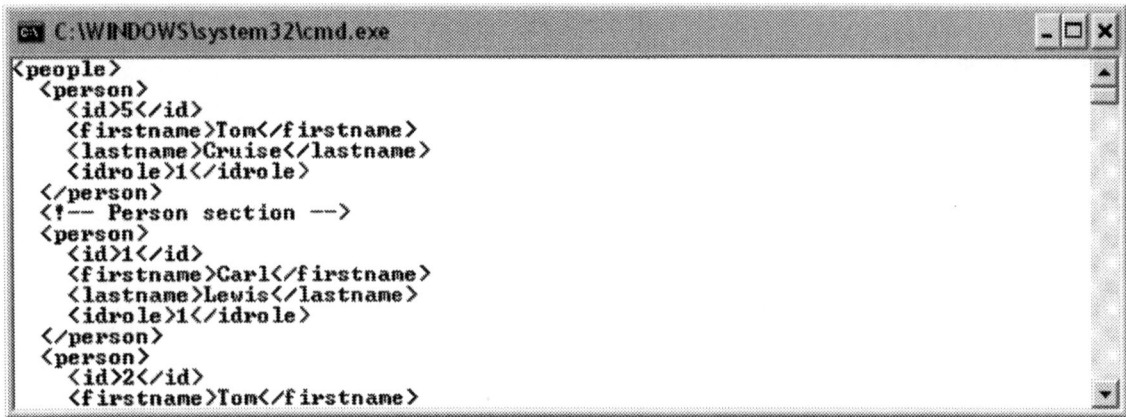

Figure 3-11. Adding a new person element at the beginning of the XML document

Using the AddAfterThis and AddBeforeThis methods after positioning the cursor at the desired node, we can add a new element after or before the current node, respectively.

Updating Elements in an XML Document

Using the SetElement method of XElement, we can update an element with a new value. In Listing 3-22 we change the description of the first role contained in the People XML document.

Listing 3-22. Using the SetElement Method to Modify an Element's Value

```
Dim xml As XElement = XElement.Load("..\..\People.xml")

Dim role As XElement = xml.Descendants("role").First()
Console.WriteLine("-=-=ORIGINAL-=-=")
Console.WriteLine(role)

role.SetElement("roledescription", "Actor")
Console.WriteLine(String.Empty)
Console.WriteLine("-=-=UPDATED-=-=")
Console.WriteLine(role)
```

After having reached the first role node, we can use the SetElement method to change the role description to the Actor. (Figure 3-12 shows the output.)

```
C:\WINDOWS\system32\cmd.exe                                      _ □ ×
-=-=ORIGINAL-=-=
<role>
  <id>1</id>
  <roledescription>Manager</roledescription>
</role>

-=-=UPDATED-=-=
<role>
  <id>1</id>
  <roledescription>Actor</roledescription>
</role>
Press any key to continue . . .
```

Figure 3-12. The SetElement method changes the value of an XML element.

Similarly, using the SetAttribute method of the XElement class we can change the value of the specified attribute. (See Listing 3-23.)

Listing 3-23. Changing the Value of an Attribute by Using the SetAttribute Method

```
Dim xml As XElement = XElement.Load("..\..\People.xml")

Dim role As XElement = xml.Descendants("idperson").First()
Console.WriteLine("-=-=ORIGINAL-=-=")
Console.WriteLine(role)

role.SetAttribute("year", "2006")
Console.WriteLine(String.Empty)
Console.WriteLine("-=-=UPDATED-=-=")
Console.WriteLine(role)
```

As you can see from the output in Figure 3-13, the year of the first idperson element is changed from 2004 to 2006.

```
C:\WINDOWS\system32\cmd.exe                                      _ □ ×
-=-=ORIGINAL-=-=
<idperson id="1" year="2004" salaryyear="10000,0000" />

-=-=UPDATED-=-=
<idperson id="1" year="2006" salaryyear="10000,0000" />
Press any key to continue . . .
```

Figure 3-13. Just like the SetElement method changes an element's value by using the SetAttribute method, it can change an attribute's value.

Note ➡ Using the SetElement and SetAttribute methods with elements and attributes not already present in an XML document is equivalent to adding them to the current element. On the other hand, specifying a null value with an existing element removes that element from the XML document.

Finally, to replace an entire section of the XML document with new values, use the ReplaceContent method of XElement, as in Listing 3-24.

Listing 3-24. Replacing a Whole XML Document Section by Using the ReplaceContent Method

```
Dim xml As XElement = XElement.Load("..\..\People.xml")

xml.Element("person").ReplaceContent(New XElement("id", 5), _
                    New XElement("firstname", "Tom"), _
                    New XElement("lastname", "Cruise"), _
                    New XElement("idrole", 1))
Console.WriteLine(xml)
```

The first person element is substituted with a new person, as shown in Figure 3-14.

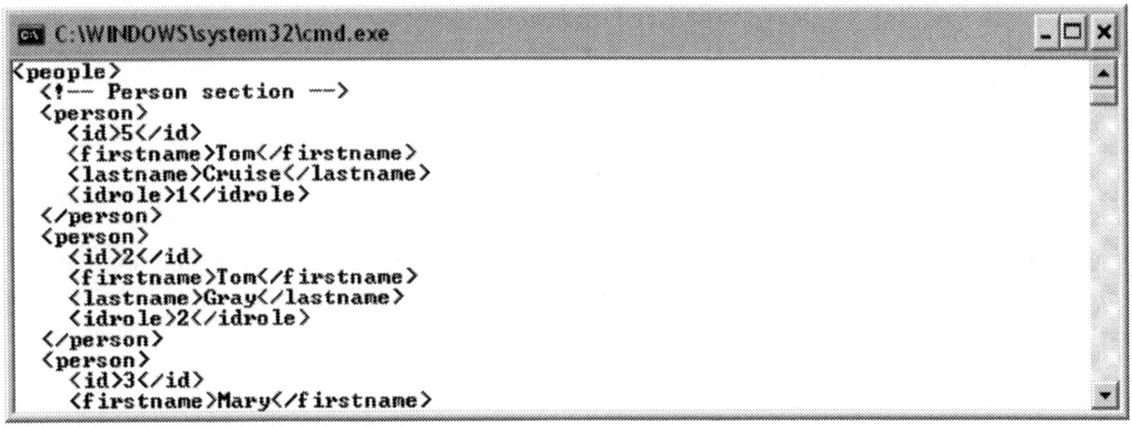

Figure 3-14. The output for Listing 3-24

Deleting Elements from an XML Document

The XElement class provides two methods to remove an element from an XML document: Remove and Remove Content.

The Remove method applied to the current node removes that element from the XML document. Using the Remove method with an IEnumerable(Of XElement) collection iterates through all the elements and removes them (see Listing 3-25).

Listing 3-25. Removing an idperson Element and the role Section

```
Dim xml As XElement = XElement.Load("..\..\People.xml")

xml.Descendants("idperson").First().Remove()

xml.Elements("role").Remove()

Console.WriteLine(xml)
```

Figure 3-15 shows the output of this code snippet.

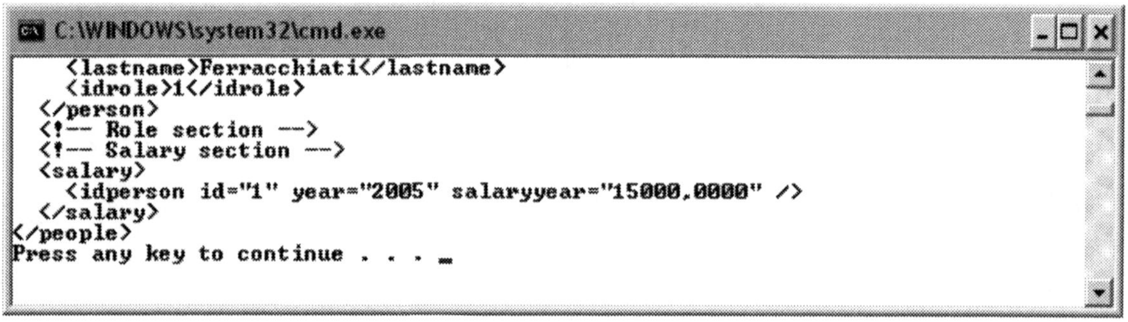

Figure 3-15. The output shows that the role section and an idperson element have been deleted.

The second removal method that XElement provides is RemoveContent, which lets you remove an entire section of an XML document. In Listing 3-26 all the content of the first role element is removed.

Listing 3-26. Removing the Content of the First role Element

```
Dim xml As XElement = XElement.Load("..\..\People.xml")

xml.Element("role").RemoveContent()

Console.WriteLine(xml)
```

As you can see from the output in Figure 3-16, the first role element loses its content and is replaced by an empty tag (<role />).

```
C:\WINDOWS\system32\cmd.exe                                    _ □ ×
 </person>
 <!-- Role section -->
 <role />
 <role>
    <id>2</id>
    <roledescription>Developer</roledescription>
 </role>
 <!-- Salary section -->
 <salary>
    <idperson id="1" year="2004" salaryyear="10000.0000" />
    <idperson id="1" year="2005" salaryyear="15000.0000" />
 </salary>
</people>
Press any key to continue . . . _
```

Figure 3-16. The RemoveContent method applied to the first role element

RemoveAttribute() called on the current element removes all its attributes. To remove just a single attribute, you have to set that attribute's value to null using the SetAttribute method, as mentioned in the note after Listing 3-23.

LINQ to XML and LINQ to SQL

The final section of this chapter covers the integration aspects between two LINQ technologies: LINQ to XML and LINQ to SQL.

In Listing 3-27 we use a LINQ to SQL query to retrieve all the person rows from the database, which produces an XML file similar to the People.xml file.

Listing 3-27. Querying the SQL Server People Database to Produce an XML Document from a LINQ to SQL Query

```
Dim people As New PeopleDataContext()

Dim xml As New XElement("people", _
            From p In people.People _
        Select New XElement("person", _
            New XElement("id", p.ID), _
            New XElement("firstname", p.FirstName), _
            New XElement("lastname", p.LastName), _
            New XElement("idrole", p.IDRole)))
Console.WriteLine(xml)

Listing3_28(xml, people)
```

Using a LINQ to SQL query as an argument to the XElement constructor, we can produce an XML document in which content comes directly from database data. Figure 3-17 shows the output of the code snippet in Listing 3-27.

```
C:\WINDOWS\system32\cmd.exe                                              _ □ ×
<people>
  <person>
    <id>1</id>
    <firstname>Carl</firstname>
    <lastname>Lewis</lastname>
    <idrole>1</idrole>
  </person>
  <person>
    <id>2</id>
    <firstname>Tom</firstname>
    <lastname>Gray</lastname>
    <idrole>2</idrole>
  </person>
  <person>
    <id>3</id>
    <firstname>Mary</firstname>
    <lastname>Grant</lastname>
    <idrole>2</idrole>
  </person>
  <person>
    <id>61</id>
    <firstname>Fabio</firstname>
    <lastname>Ferracchiati</lastname>
    <idrole>1</idrole>
  </person>
</people>
Press any key to continue . . .
```

Figure 3-17. The XML document produced by querying the People database

Now consider taking an XML document as the data source and querying the database to search for new rows. If the XML document contains new rows not present in the database, the code in Listing 3-28 uses LINQ to SQL to add them to the database.

Note ➡ To execute the code shown in Listing 3-28 you have to leave the code of Listing 3-27 uncommented. That's because the code in Listing 3-28 simply adds a new record into the xml object retrieved by the code in Listing 3-27.

Listing 3-28. Searching for New Records in an XML Document and Eventually Adding Them to the Database

```
Sub Listing3_28(ByVal xml As XElement, ByVal people As PeopleDataContext)
    xml.Add(New XElement("person", _
            New XElement("id", 5), _
            New XElement("firstname", "Tom"), _
            New XElement("lastname", "Cruise"), _
            New XElement("idrole", 1)))

    Console.WriteLine(xml)

    AddPerson(xml, people)

End Sub
```

Using the XML document created in Listing 3-27, the code adds a new person element and passes the final XElement object to the AddPerson method that checks the XML document for new records, eventually adding them to the database. Listing 3-29 shows the code of the AddPerson method.

Listing 3-29. Adding a New Person Record, Read from the XML Document, That Is Not Already Present in the Database

```
Dim people = xml.Descendants("person")
Dim id As Integer

For Each Dim person In people
    id = Convert.ToInt32(person.Element("id").Value)

    Dim query = From p In peopledb.People _
        Where p.ID = id _
        Select p

    If query.ToList().Count = 0  Then
        Dim per As New Person()
        per.FirstName = person.Element("firstname").Value
        per.LastName = person.Element("lastname").Value
        per.IDRole = person.Element("idrole").Value
        peopledb.People.Add(per)
    End If
Next
```

```
peopledb.SubmitChanges()
```

The body of the AddPerson method retrieves the collection of person elements in the XML document:

```
Dim people = xml.Descendants("person")
```

Then it iterates through the collection and queries the People table by primary key for each person:

```
Dim query = From p In peopledb.People _
    Where p.ID = id _
    Select p
```

If the collection produced by the ToList method doesn't contain items, then the person is not in the table; in that case, a new Person object is created, filled with values read from the XML document, and added to People.

Once all the XML elements have been processed, the insertions are propagated to the database with SubmitChanges().

Summary

You've seen that querying an XML document with LINQ to XML is easy and requires little more than knowledge of LINQ query syntax. You no longer have to be an expert in XML to handle XML data easily. You can focus on what you want to do rather than on how to do it!

Moreover, you've seen how LINQ to XML allows you to easily create XML documents and modify their contents.

We've reached the end of the chapter, as well as the end of the book. You've seen all the major features of a great new technology, LINQ, that is still in beta but it is already mature enough to be used in applications. LINQ is the future of .NET data access—and the future is now.